WHAT IT TAKES
(FOR A WOMAN)
TO MAKE A LIVING
AND HOLD ON TO MONEY.

MONEY
MANAGEMENT
FOR WOMEN

"The woman who enters the economic world often finds she really knows very little about what makes it work and what does not work for her. Ms. Rosalie Minkow takes her through a maze of hazards and pitfalls, describing what it takes to make a living and hold on to money, facing the tribulations of taxes, illness, divorce, widowhood and prospective retirement, even to thoughts of providing an estate. Here is a handy primer for the uninitiated—male or female—about the problems, pressures and power of money in a world that measures most things by it."
—The Digest of Investment Advices

MONEY
MANAGEMENT
☐ FOR ☐
WOMEN
ROSALIE MINKOW

PLAYBOY
PAPERBACKS

Published simultaneously in the United States and Canada by Playboy Paperbacks, New York, New York. Printed in the United States of America. Library of Congress Catalog Card Number: 80-84373. First edition.

Books are available at quantity discounts for promotional and industrial use. For further information, write to Premium Sales, Playboy Paperbacks, 1633 Broadway, New York, New York 10019.

ISBN: 0-872-16816-6

First printing May 1981.

This book is dedicated to my husband,
Howard Minkow

Contents

8 CONTENTS

Money Management
for Women

Voltaire said: "When it is a question of money, everybody is of the same religion." What he should have appended to that is: "But not everybody is of the same sex."

Men have had a head start on women in knowledge and experience in the area of money management. But women are now a major force in today's economy—as earners, consumers, and investors.
Consider these statistics:

- Life insurance coverage in force for women rose 90 percent, from $200 billion to $380 billion, between 1970 and 1976.
- Individual women holders of American Express credit cards rose 171 percent in six years, from 700,000 in 1972 to 1.9 million in 1978.
- According to the New York Stock Exchange, women represent 50.3 percent of all adult stockholders. About 12 million women own stock or mutual-fund shares.
- The U.S. Labor Department says women make up almost half of the work force and bring

home paychecks totaling $250 billion or more each year.
- Enrollment in colleges and universities is now 50 percent female.
- Women control the spending of almost half a trillion dollars a year.

Still, the average woman lags behind the average man in financial expertise. The aim of this book is to clue you in on money so that you will have a chance of catching up. It will help you to unclutter and to organize your personal financial life and will teach you some of those tricks and techniques that men have known for years.

The first step in organizing your personal financial life is to determine your net worth. The next chapter will show you how.

You May Be Worth
More Than You Think

How much are you worth? At times you might feel you're not worth a plugged nickel. Your stack of bills looks higher than the number in your checking account balance. On top of that, you didn't get that raise you expected, or your business is off.

But wait—are you really taking a realistic view of your personal balance sheets or assets and liabilities? You may be worth more than you think. You can only find out by taking a personal inventory. A personal balance sheet not only tells you where you are now but also gives you a good account of where you are going. You may find that you need to reorder your priorities to achieve a greater feeling of financial security.

With today's rampant inflation, you need to make a periodic assessment of your net worth. Your house may have increased tremendously in value. Add to that the value of your car and other material goods, and you may find that you are now in the category wherein, if you die, your estate will be taxed. That tax bite begins at approximately $200,000 if you are single and $400,000 if you are married. If you find after your calculations that your estate would be bitten badly by taxes, you might like to make adjustments such as segregating assets between wife's and husband's, gifting during your lifetime, revising wills taking into account the advantages of trusts, or insuring the payment of the possible tax liability.

A periodic assessment of your net worth also determines whether the amount of life insurance you are carrying is sufficient to take care of those you leave behind. And what about home insurance? Could you replace your home at current value? Then, too, there is the matter of planning your retirement. Will you have a realistic retirement income with your present plan of investments, savings, etc., or do you see that you have to make adjustments in your retirement planning? Other financial objectives are an adequate emergency fund and an education fund for children.

An annual checkup on your net worth will show you specifically where you are going. Some loans will be reduced or paid off. The market value of your cars will change. The value of your silver and jewelry may increase. Your pension profit sharing plan usually rises.

How do you go about making up a personal balance sheet? Very much the same way large corporations do. You tally up your total assets and then your liabilities to outsiders. The resulting difference will give you the answer to how much you are worth. Just as large corporations do, you will want to make your assessment as of the same time each year. Many people find it convenient to make their calculations before April 15 when they are digging through financial records for tax purposes; it is only a little more effort to take the next step and make a private economic appraisal.

The personal balance sheet differs from the corporation balance sheet in one important way. The corporate balance sheet balances evenly—with assets matching liabilities—while the personal balance sheet in most cases does not. If your assets just balanced your liabilities, your net worth would be zero—obviously not a desirable condition. In the case of corporate balance sheets, the difference between assets and liabilities to outsiders goes to stockholders for amounts called capital stock earned surplus, capital surplus, or retained earnings. The stockholders are owners of the company, and hence they own its net worth or whatever is the difference between total assets and the liabilities due to outsiders.

When figuring your assets, put down the market value of what they would bring if they were sold on the day you make your assessment. You may have put $10,000 into a mutual fund, but if it is now worth only $7,000, that's all you would get if you sell. You may want to have silver and jewelry appraised for an absolutely accurate tally, but by reading the newspaper ads, you will get a general idea of their value.

Net Worth Statement as of _____
                                                (date)

Assets
    Cash on hand
    Checking account balance
    Savings account
    Notes and mortgages held
    Loans to individuals
    Stocks and bonds
        Common stocks
        Preferred stocks
        Bonds
    Real estate owned

Life insurance (cash value)
>Policies owned by husband—type of policy, face amount beneficiary, net cash value
>Policies owned by wife—type of policy, face amount beneficiary, net cash value

Pension plan

Business interests (such as partnership equities valuation of closely held corporations)

Other property
>Car or cars—book value
>House furnishings
>Jewelry, silver
>Collections (such as stamps or coins)

Liabilities
Loans
>Bank loans
>Car loans
>Personal loans

House mortgage

Taxes due
>Income taxes
>>Federal
>>State
>Other taxes (such as real estate)
>Personal business taxes

Pledges
>Church or synagogue
>College
>Other charities

Children's allowances

Department store and credit card bills outstanding

Other bills outstanding

Contingent liabilities (such as co-maker or co-endorser of someone else's note, or the balance of a lease on rented premises)

After listing amounts of assets and amounts of liabilities in two separate columns, total each. The difference between total assets and total amount owed (or liabilities) is your net worth. Not only will you have a picture of your net worth, you will be able to see what you own and what areas you are strong or weak in. You may find, for instance, that your house is worth more than you had imagined and that your house insurance is not adequate to replace it in case of a fire. You will want to increase your home insurance coverage. You may find that you are heavy in jewelry but too light in life insurance. Thus you may decide to sell off some jewelry and put the cash toward purchase of another life insurance policy.

Monthly reconciliation of your checking account is essential to good personal financial organization. The next chapter tells you how to reconcile and how to easily detect and correct errors.

3

Expert Tips on Reconciling
Your Bank Statement

It's a warm, wonderful feeling when, on your first try at reconciliation, your checkbook and your bank statement agree. On the other hand, when the two don't match, it may mean hours of teeth-gnashing frustration and a grubby-looking checkbook.

What should you do when you have trouble reconciling bank statements? Here are some helpful tips offered by skilled accountants.

First, *don't delay reconciling*. This is important; do it as soon as possible after the statement arrives. Take the statement's balance and add all deposits and subtract all checks that have not cleared as of the statement date. Subtract bank service charges and any other charges automatically deducted from your checking account from your checkbook balance. Your bank statement figure should be comparable to that in your checkbook.

Supposing you have done all this, yet your figure still disagrees with the bank's? *Important*: Do *not* make erasures or corrections in your checkbook as you find errors. This very often leads to further errors and confusion all the way through your checkbook. Instead, find errors first and note them on separate sheets of paper. (You will deal with this later.)

Here is how errors are commonly found:

1. Start by looking for obvious omissions by you or the bank. Go through your pile of checks, which should have been sorted in order of date written. As you turn over each check, put a check mark next to the item in your checkbook. You may find that you have forgotten to account for an outstanding check or that you wrote the check for a different amount from that on your stub. Also compare the amount you have written on the check with what is recorded by the bank as their payment in the lower right-hand corner of the check—or, if your bank is not computerized, compare it with the bank's itemization on the statement to see that both figures agree. Remember that banks are run by human beings, and they make mistakes, too.

2. Look for checks or amounts erroneously debited to your account by the bank for various reasons: similarity of name with another depositor's, confusion of your bank account number with someone else's, etc.

3. See if you forgot to deduct noncheck items from your checkbook: insurance payments, loan payments, savings plans, etc., automatically deducted from your account.

4. Now look at your deposits. Perhaps you neglected to record a deposit in your checkbook. Compare the bank's deposits column with what you have recorded. For deposits made after the date of your bank statement that you might have forgotten to record in your checkbook, hunt up your bank deposit slips to check the date and amount.

5. If, after checking out the aforementioned potentialities of error, you still have a difference in your reconciliation, subtract the two numbers: your adjusted bank statement and your checkbook balance. Working

with this difference, you may now be able to find your errors.

A difference of 1 or 2 in any column of figures is probably an addition error. Re-add all figures in your checkbook.

If the difference is divisible by 2, chances are you added instead of subtracted or vice versa. Look for the one-half amount in the column of checks drawn or deposits made.

If the difference of your bank statement and checkbook balance is divisible by 9, you may have transposed figures somewhere (written the figures in the wrong order). Example: Your bank statement shows a balance of $1,521. Your checkbook balance is $1,251. The difference between the two numbers is 270. The 270 is divisible by 9, which means you may have a transposition somewhere. How to find your error? The number that results from dividing 270 by 9 is 3, which is also the difference between the transposed numbers: the 5 and 2 in your original figures. The zero tells you that the transposition was between the second and third digits of some number in your checkbook or bank statement. It may be a check, a deposit, or a forwarded balance error. If your quotient had had one digit, the transposition would have been between the last two numbers; if it had had three digits, it would have been between the third and fourth digits.

If the difference between your checkbook balance and your bank statement is divisible by 9 or 99, it could also be what is called a "one-column" or "two-column" slide." You wrote the right digits, but your decimal point was in the wrong place. Example: You wrote $36.90 for $3.69 or $369.00. See if there is an amount with those numbers in it in your checkbook and bank statement. Compare to see if the error is yours or the bank's.

If, after covering all these possibilities, you still find yourself with a difference, make a comparison sheet against the bank's statement. On a separate sheet of paper, list all the checks you have written for the period of reconciliation. Total them up. List all deposits for the period. Total them up. Add and subtract them from your opening balance. Compare the result with your bank statement. You should be able to localize the errors.

Now that you have found your errors, corrections may be made.

First, list all errors, marking them plus or minus on the checkbook page of your reconciliation point. The list of errors corrected should be the same as your difference.

Then note your difference at the end of your period of reconciliation in your checkbook. Next, adjust your last figure in the checkbook by that difference so that the balance is now corrected as at the end of that date. Example: You found the following errors: a transposition of $45 in your favor; an omission of a $25 check written to the supermarket; a deposit added incorrectly, giving you $100 more than you had originally accounted for; a bank charge of $2.93 not deducted. Instead of making numerous erasures, you adjust and note your errors at checkbook page of date of reconciliation, as follows:

Transposition	+	$ 45.00
Supermarket	—	25.00
Deposit 11/2/80	+	100.00
Bank charge	—	2.93
	+	$117.07

Add $117.07 to your balance on the page of the date of reconciliation. Then add $117.07 to your last figure in your checkbook balance.

Now that you know your net worth and how to reconcile your checking account properly, you should think in terms of a budget, even though we are living in inflationary times. Chapter 4 tells how to do it.

4

Budgeting for
Inflationary Times

Budgeting during inflationary times sounds impossible and dreary. Actually, it is more important than ever to budget to keep out of debt. As for being dreary, what could be drearier than having to give up vacation plans because you just do not have the money to do more than sit under a sun lamp?

Think of a budget as a tool to help you spend wisely and reach your goals. Implementation of a budget will pinpoint negative spending habits so that you can change them and direct spending toward your ends.

Financial goals will differ according to your life stage. A young woman's priority might be a vacation in a place where she will meet people and enhance her social life. Later, she might marry and have a joint goal with her husband to save for the birth of a child. Later, a chief goal might be saving for children's college education. Still later, saving for retirement might be the chief financial goal.

Budgets should be geared to your life style, too. It might be more important to you to do a great deal of entertaining than to drive a late-model car. Training courses might be more important to you than a large closet full of clothes. Buying flowering plants at a nursery might be more exciting for you than an evening of dinner and theater. Your life style is like no one else's, so you cannot borrow any old budget and expect it to fit, just as you cannot expect to slip into any old pair of shoes and expect them to fit.

There are some factors to keep in mind before setting up your budget. Your spending motives should be based on what will enrich your life and not on what will produce what you think are favorable reactions in others. Under this category comes buying extravagant presents for people in order to impress them or get them to like you. It also means not buying what everyone else has just to feel "in." Why must you pay $150 for a handbag because it has those coveted designer initials when you can go to a discount handbag place and find just as good quality for much less? Dare to be different. Who knows? Everyone may be following your style in a short while.

Another factor to keep in mind is that time is money. Running from store to store for bargains not only uses up gas or fare money, it uses up time. Consider whether you might be better off using the time by taking on a free-lance project that will increase your income. On the other hand, some people consider shopping a form of recreation, so that time is considered their fun time. To each her own!

How do you start figuring your budget? The first step is to estimate what your income will be for a year, since most budgets cover a twelve-month period. You might want your budget to coincide with the tax year because when you are organizing your records for tax forms, you will find it simpler to take the extra step and set up a budget.

If this is your first budget, you might want to set up a

three-month trial plan. After you see how the trial period goes, you can revise it to cover a longer period.

Write down all funds that you expect to receive during your planning period. Start with fixed amounts that you get regularly: your salary, your spouse's salary, alimony, special allowance or benefits, and any other regular payments to you. Then put down the variables that you expect—interest from savings accounts and bonds, dividends from stocks, rents, gifts, and money from other sources.

If your earnings are irregular, base your income estimate on your previous income and solid current prospects. If your income fluctuates sharply—if you are an actress, a seasonal worker, or a saleswoman on commission, for example—then work with the smallest figure that you can expect. You can always put money into savings or revise your budget if your income rises.

Now list fixed monthly expenses—those that you have little control over: mortgage payments or rent, transportation to work, utilities, installment payments on old debts. Next, make a list of the flexible expenses: food and beverages, household operation and maintenance, furnishings, clothing, personal-care services and items, entertainment, and any others you may incur for your life style. You can come up with monthly figures for these items by keeping close track of them for three months and then figuring average monthly costs.

Certain expenses, such as insurance premiums, taxes, car insurance, and Christmas gifts, are seasonal rather than month-to-month expenses. Create a seasonal fund for them on your monthly budget by figuring your costs for them and dividing by twelve. You should put enough aside into your seasonal fund each month so that those bills do not come as "shockers."

You also want to have a fund for savings and investment money. Ten percent of your salary should go in this fund every month. This fund will take care of emergencies such as unexpected car repair or medical or dental bills, and a portion of it—however much you determine you will need—should go toward fulfilling your long-term goals.

Budget	Amount per Month
Income from all sources	$
Emergency and future-goals savings	$
Seasonal expenses allotment	$
Regular monthly expenses:	
Rent or mortgage	$
Utilities	$
Transportation to work	$
Installments on loans; other debts	$
Any other fixed monthly expense	$
Total fixed expenses	$
Flexible expenses:	$
Food and beverages	$
Household operation and maintenance	$
Furnishings and equipment	$
Clothing	$
Personal care	$
Medical care	$
Entertainment	$
Contributions and gifts	$
Total flexible expenses	$
Grand total of savings and expenses	$

If your income and expenses balance, fine. If your income exceeds your expenses, even better. You may want to increase the amount you are putting toward your goals or raise your standards for your monthly categories. You can afford to go to the theater more often. You can afford to eat meat more often. You may even be able to afford sable instead of mink!

However, with most of us, our expenses outstrip our income. One solution is to increase income. If you are an unemployed wife, it may be time to take on a full- or part-time job. Your children might baby-sit, deliver newspapers, mow lawns, or work part-time after school for spending money and to pay, say, for some of their clothing. If you are already employed, you may consider taking on a second job, but you must take care that your moonlighting or free-lancing does not put such a strain on you that you wind up paying out increased income to doctors.

Beware the effect of double-digit inflation on your purchasing dollar and when considering increasing your income. You might think that you are keeping up if your income increases to a rate equal to inflation. This is not true, because you pay income tax on the money you earn.

If expenses exceed income, it is also a mandate to adjust your budget to reduce expenditures in some of the categories. You might exchange a large car for a smaller, more gas-efficient one. Even better, you could turn in your car for a bicycle and rent a car for long-distance trips. You may decide that you can move into a studio apartment and with clever screening of various areas have almost as much privacy as with a one-bedroom apartment at less rent. You might save by converting endowment to a cheaper form of insurance.

Are you deep in debt? Resist taking out a loan to

consolidate your debts. The loan will only make you feel better temporarily as you pay off the small bills. However, what you are probably left with is loan payments at a higher rate of interest than that on your small bills and for a longer period. Much better to "level" with your creditors. After all, the people to whom you owe money are chiefly interested in getting their money, not in suing you. They also know that everyone gets into a pickle once in a while. Better to calmly explain the situation to your creditors as soon as you discover yourself in it.

Make a list of your creditors. Note how much you owe to each of them. Then make a careful analysis of your income and savings. Work out how much you can afford to pay each of them on an installment basis. This sort of figuring will keep your credit standing from going down the drain. (If you lose your credit standing, it could take years to get it back.)

Write each creditor a letter. Simply state that you have a financial crisis. Ask whether they would accept payment in installments. The installment amounts that you decide on should not be so high that you would have to default on them (in which case, you really lose your credibility). Most creditors will accept your offer. Again, they will be more willing to compromise with you than to sue you for nonpayment. Try to make your offer before your creditors are angered by your not answering demands for payment.

Okay, say you have cleared up all your debts. How do you avoid getting into that situation again? Planning your financial goals and setting priorities and keeping them firmly in mind will help. For example, suppose you would love to furnish your dining area. You saw a butcher block table and cane chairs—perfect! Instead of charging the set then and there and paying installment payments with interest, put money aside each month in your savings fund and pay for it outright. In case you are tempted to charge it so that it will be yours right then and there, figure out how much those interest payments are going to cost. Most likely you will be happier, and really feel smug, if you save up first and plunk the entire amount down before the set is delivered. By the way, don't forget to include the amount for sales tax when you are saving up for a large purchase like a dining set; sales tax can add a hefty amount to the cost.

Include in your savings an emergency fund so that you are not put into debt by unexpected auto repairs or hospital bills. Three times your monthly salary should be earmarked for an emergency fund.

Beware impulse buying. If you know you are an impulse buyer, shop with your husband or a friend who is able to provide the strength to help you avoid buying superfluous items. Some people leave their credit cards and checkbooks at home unless they are planning to make a specific purchase. Others shop with a list and stick to it. They don't even look at anything that is not on the list.

If you do buy something on silly impulse and realize when you get home that it is an extravagance, rectify your mistake. Return the item before you rationalize a need for it. And don't be embarrassed with the salesperson or feel sorry about returning it. Salespeople are very used to returns.

Another attitude that can keep you broke is the desire to "keep up with the Joneses." This can be a quick way to waste money or run into financial trouble. Trying to live beyond your means by trying to keep up with more affluent neighbors or friends can be a real temptation. Part of the solution is to live in the kind of neighborhood that is within your living and earning standards or to acquire new friends who are not so concerned with material goods and spending. Also, perhaps you need to tell yourself that people should like you for what you are rather than what you have. As for entertaining, wouldn't you rather have a simple spaghetti dinner with interesting company than pheasant and caviar with dull company?

Failure to estimate accurately the costs that are associated with major purchases can also lead to debt. Let's say you and your husband have decided to buy a home. You have enough money for that ivy-covered cottage. You have the down payment and your mortgage is okayed. Have you also included in your move to the house closing costs, maintenance costs, additional furnishings, real estate taxes, the need for another car or for paying higher transportation costs to work? If you do not make valid assessment of related costs, then you may find yourself short of funds. This may necessitate borrowing money and paying unexpected interest fees.

Learning to use credit wisely will help keep you out of debt. As we said before, if you find it difficult to resist temptation, leave your credit cards and checkbook home except when shopping for specific items. Credit cards can be a convenience if you don't abuse them. It is easier to make exchanges or returns at a department store if you use the store's card. Gasoline credit cards make it easier to keep better records for tax purposes, and of course, if you do a great deal of business entertaining, credit cards are also helpful in keeping tax records.

Do try to pay your charges on time. If you don't pay an outstanding balance when it is due, say after twenty-five or thirty days, a finance charge is assessed. This can amount to from 1 to 1½ percent monthly or 12 to 18 percent yearly.

Try to get the most for your money. You can really enjoy yourself if you regard this as a challenge. Take food shopping, for instance. Food is a major spending category. It has risen drastically with inflation, and food is one thing we cannot do without. But we can still stay within reasonable limits with "the supermarket smarts":

1. Check newspaper ads and supermarket displays for special prices.

2. Clip coupons and trade off with friends the coupons you don't use for those they can't use but you can.

3. Buy food in season. The food pages of your newspaper will tell you what's in season and when.

4. Always look at unit prices. If unit prices are not stated on the shelf under the items, consider bringing along a hand calculator and figuring the unit price yourself.

5. Avoid convenience foods if you can. Don't buy the frozen vegetables with butter sauce when you can easily add butter or margarine yourself. But do keep some convenience food in the house. It can be cheaper than grabbing a bite out when you are too tired or rushed to cook.

6. Try to do your supermarket shopping all at once, once a week. We know if we go into a supermarket for one item, we never come out with just one, and usually the extra items are ones we don't really need.

7. When you go to the supermarket, bring a list

and stick to it. It helps to plan a week's menus in advance and buy all the ingredients for your week's menus so that you won't have to make another trip. Tip: Make a list of items you need on the back of a used business envelope. Tuck coupons for items on the list into the envelope. Another tip: Keeping food costs down can sometimes result in dull eating. Include one surprise treat for yourself and your family in your weekly shopping, such as a package of a brand-new cookie to sample. Still another tip: If your husband and children are like ours, leave them home when you shop the supermarket. Husbands get lost in the beer department and children in the candy department.

For other needs, do try to shop the sales. For example, before the August white sales, take a survey of your linen closet. Calculate how many sheets and pillow cases you will need to replace worn ones, and with the fall and winter holidays in mind, plan your purchases of tablecloths. Glassware, silver, furniture, and clothing also have special sale times. Watch the ads for notices of sales.

If you are looking for a new sofa, you can find one at substantial savings at furniture outlet stores. There may be a scratch in the wood or a small tear in the fabric, but the substantial saving and your ability to refinish or mend can more than compensate.

One friend of ours who had her heart set on an antique wood music stand, but found them all way over her head in price, took an adult-education course in woodworking and made a copy of an antique stand that had caught her fancy. Do-it-yourselfers can save money by studying plumbing repair, auto maintenance, reupholstering, patternmaking, and other skills.

If you have a regular savings plan, fine. If you don't and have trouble disciplining yourself for saving, you might try one or more of these tips:

1. Have your payroll department deduct a certain amount from your paycheck and put it directly into a savings account *before* you are paid.
2. Save your extra earnings—overtime, free-lance work, moonlighting job.
3. Don't spend your next raise for a few months after you get it. Pretend you are still earning your previous wage and deposit the extra money.
4. After a loan is repaid, such as a car loan, continue setting aside the same amount of money as the loan payments and put it into a savings account.

At the end of your trial three-month budget period, compare what you spent with what you planned to spend. If your spending was quite different from your plan, find out why. Perhaps you fritter away money without knowing where it really goes. Try carrying a small notebook in your purse and write down every dime you spend for a few weeks: cigarettes, coffee breaks, sodas, magazines. After a month, total the amounts. These money leaks can add up to quite a bit, and very probably you are not enjoying spending money on them as much as if you saved the money for, say, a special designer dress that you might wear time and again, really getting your money's worth.

A budget is something that needs working on. If you

did not succeed with your first budget, analyze it and see where it needs adjusting. A budget should fit you and satisfy your individual needs. Do not expect to have a perfect budget the first time you set one up. Keep working at it and remember that even a perfect budget must be changed from time to time as circumstances change and new goals are set.

You may find if you are not working that your budget will only be balanced if you get out in the work world. The next few chapters will tell you how to set your sights on a career and, if you already have one, how to get promotions and raises.

5

Choosing a Career

A recent Department of Labor survey showed that nine out of ten women will work outside the home at some time in their lives. Another survey conducted by the Gallup Poll for the White House Conference on Families revealed that one-third of the women polled wanted to combine having a family with a full-time job outside the home.

Some women work for subsistence. Their salaries are needed to provide food, clothing, and shelter for themselves and possibly a family. They may be the sole support or a necessary second salary providing for a family's bare necessities. Other women are fortunate enough to be able to regard work as more than a necessity for subsistence. For them, work also represents status, achievement, creativity, and self-satisfaction.

These women do more than work at a job. They are building a career. What is the difference between a job and a career? A job is a short-term money-earning, limited-horizons stint. A career may consist of a series of jobs each leading to five-, ten-, twenty-, and thirty-year or lifetime goals. A career usually requires extensive soul searching of values and interests, and training.

It is revealing that men more frequently think in terms of "career" rather than "job." Perhaps that is the main reason men's salaries average so much higher than women's. Men are less willing to "settle."

The young woman who is starting out on her first job, the mature woman who is reentering the world of work, the woman who is dissatisfied with her work and would like to make a change—all must take time out to evaluate just what it is that they want out of life. Is your goal to make a lot of money? Enough to buy a home? To be able to take lavish vacations? To dine at four-star restaurants? Or does success spell power to you? To be chairman of the board? To be quoted by business editors of metropolitan dailies? To be invited to a White House conference on your specialty? Or does success mean to you limiting your work goals, but having in return enough time to spend with family and friends?

What about your interests? Do you enjoy public speaking? Writing reports? Sketching imaginative designs? Soothing the sick?

How are your work habits? Do you work best alone or with people? Are you competitive? Do you enjoy taking the full responsibility for decisions and directing others?

What is your education? Did you finish high school? Did you have only some college or did you get your degree? Did you do graduate work? What were you most interested in and what was your best subject in school?

What about volunteer work? Were you always the president of your organization? Did you enjoy doing PR or working on the newsletter? Were you the one who was invariably chosen to speak for your organization?

Do you have a special talent? Do you design your own clothing? Make your own car repairs? Bake infallible pie crusts?

You can ask yourself these and similar questions or go to a reputable career counseling service that will administer psychological tests to measure your values, interests, aptitudes, and personality traits. If you go to a career counseling service, you still have to decide among several occupations for which the service will conclude you are best suited. Furthermore, no service can measure whether you have the drive to be successful in a specific field. Only you can determine that. Why not save yourself money and time and try to come to a conclusion about your career goal yourself? No one knows you as well as you do, providing you are objective and honest. If you find this too difficult, then by all means do use the professional career consultant. (Look in the Yellow Pages under "Vocational Guidance.")

In this search for a career, your librarian may be your best friend. He or she can pull books from the shelves that are all about career choosing. Many libraries even have career counselors to help you explore career possibilities. Call your local library and ask if it has such a service, which in most cases is free.

If you are determined to go the whole route yourself on this career planning business, your next step involves the library, too. That is where you should find the *Dictionary of Occupational Titles*, called the "DOT" by those in the "know." It is a detailed analysis by the Department of Labor of over twenty thousand jobs.

The DOT is your bridge in the job matching process. Think of yourself as a computer. Inside you is the result of your soul searching for your goals, interests, work habits, education, what you enjoyed in volunteer work, your special talents, etc. In light of this input, turn to the various occupations that you feel might interest you. Match your input with the job classification lead statement that comes closest. The DOT's occupational definitions are written in broad terms reflecting the most typical characteristics of a job as it occurs in the American economy.

In order to present the millions of jobs in the U.S. economy in an organized way, the DOT groups jobs into "occupations" according to their similarities and defines the structure and content of all listed occupations. Occupational definitions are the result of comprehensive studies of how similar jobs are performed in establishments all over the nation and are composites of data collected from diverse sources. The term "occupation" as used in the DOT refers to this collective description of a number of individual jobs performed with minor variations in many establishments.

Let's take an example to illustrate how you might use the DOT. Suppose you enjoy writing. You write frequent witty notes to friends. You volunteered to write the newsletter for your church, and enjoyed doing it. You always made top grades in English in college and were particularly good at creative writing.

You turn to the DOT's page on Occupations in Writing. Underneath this group is a description in broad terms of all writing occupations. Because you do not wish to be an author struggling alone on a manuscript that may lead to little or no money—you want to work with people and receive handsome remuneration—you zero in on COPYWRITER.

You see that you will be working with other people: the sales force and marketing representatives. The job requires some research, not too unlike that required for some of your college English papers. It requires you to formulate a presentation approach on products. You could draw on your experience as a homemaker who did the buying for your family by asking yourself what sales approach was successful in making its appeal to you.

The job description says that you may have to write articles, bulletins, sales letters, speeches, and other related informative and promotional material. There's where your volunteer work experience has shown that it is something you can do and enjoy doing.

Copy Writer is a job that fits your interests and needs. But what are your chances of finding employment? For the answer to that you turn to your library again and ask to see the *Occupational Outlook Handbook,* another publication from the Department of Labor, put out by its Bureau of Labor Statistics. It will tell you more about what the job is like, what education and training are necessary, and what the advancement possibilities, earnings, and employment outlook are likely to be.

Continuing our example, you zero in on Advertising Workers. You read that those employed in advertising agencies are heavily concentrated in New York City, Los Angeles, and Chicago. You don't live near any of those cities and it's not possible for you to relocate. However, you read on and learn that many manufacturing firms, retail stores, banks, power companies, professional and trade associations, and other organizations have advertising departments. There's a big field for you right in your own backyard! You learn that most employers prefer college graduates; some want advertising or business majors, but you are relieved to see that others prefer graduates with a liberal arts background such as literature. Good! You majored in English lit. You also learn that some firms have programs to train their employees in all aspects of advertising work. You decide to try for one of those firms. Reading on, you see that you must be able to take criticism. As a housewife, you have never had to deal with review of your work. You decide that you will have to learn to be objective about criticism. Perhaps an adult education writing course in which your work is subject to review by other students will help you to learn to handle criticism.

Moving on, you find that opportunities for advancement in this field are excellent for creative, talented, and hardworking people and that the prognosis for the field through the mid-1980s is healthy. Average salaries are high.

Had you researched the opportunities for teaching English, on the other hand, the handbook would have told you that employment opportunities are sparse, something of which—if you are aware of employment trends as reported in the newspapers—you would already have known, too.

In choosing copywriter over English teacher, you are also avoiding a "female ghetto" occupation—one of those occupations to which women have traditionally clung. They are jobs that are scarce and relatively low-paid. Unfortunately, in spite of the numbers of them enrolled in law and medical schools, women generally cling to traditional female-intensive professions. The result is that, according to 1978 figures compiled by the U.S. Census Bureau, the average female college graduate working full-time earned 60 percent of the salary of a man with the same education working full-time.

If you would earn as much as a man of your background, you must go where men work. In orienting your thinking toward traditionally male jobs, concentrate on the woman's angle. For instance: Criminal law might be just right for a woman because women have always been better at using psychological maneuvers to bring people around to their way of thinking—quite an attribute in winning over a jury. That's just one example. There are many others. No doubt with thought you will come up with a woman's angle for the traditionally masculine-oriented field you would like to enter.

Once you have decided on your career field, how do you go about finding a job in it? Experts say that the informal job search is the most effective. It includes direct application to employers with or without referral by friends or relatives. Locate a firm that might employ you and file an application even though you do not know for certain that an opening exists.

You can find targets for your informal search in several ways. The Yellow Pages and local Chambers of Commerce will give you the names and addresses of appropriate firms in your area. You can also get listings of most firms in a specific industry by consulting one of the industry directories on the reference shelf of your public library. Friends and relatives may suggest places to apply for a job, and people you meet in the course of your job search are also likely to give you ideas.

"Help Wanted" ads in major newspapers will contain job listings in your field. As a job search tool, they have two advantages: They are cheap and easy to acquire, and they often result in successful placement. Want ads do not have complete descriptions of the job or working conditions and pay, so you must follow them up to get that information. Keep these suggestions in mind:

- Don't rely exclusively on want ads. Use your other leads, too.

- Answer ads promptly. The opening may be filled before the ad stops running.
- Follow the ads attentively. Check them every day as early as possible to give yourself the best advantage over other applicants.
- Don't expect too much from "blind ads" that do not reveal the employer's identity. Employers use "blind ads" to avoid being swamped with applicants or to fill a particular vacancy quietly and confidentially. The chances of finding a job through "blind ads" tend to be slim.
- Be cautious about answering "no experience necessary" ads. Most employers are able to fill job openings that do not require experience without advertising in the newspaper. This type of job may mean that the job is hard to fill because of low wages or poor working conditions, or because it is straight commission work.

State employment agencies and community employment agencies may be helpful in your job search. Employers often list openings with them, and they are also helpful in providing suggestions for training programs and other ways of preparing for a particular occupation, or in simply advising you on compiling a résumé.

Private employment agencies are also sources for jobs. You will find them listed in the classified ads or the telephone book Yellow Pages and in trade journals. If you are applying for a particular advertised job, the agency will arrange an interview if they feel you are qualified or may suggest alternative openings if you are not. Find out before you use an agency whether their fee is paid by you or the employer after a successful job match is made.

College career planning and placement offices are another source of help. They offer supportive services in job seeking and a list of openings with employers who have registered with them. Many industry recruiters use college placement offices in filling their jobs.

6

Job Hunting

Before you go out on your job hunt, you will have to have a supply of résumés. We don't intend to go into detail about how to write the résumé—there are plenty of books on public library shelves to tell you that. We will just discuss a few points.

Forget about splashy beige-colored stationery with your name in maroon script. You may feel it is distinctive and makes your résumé stand out from the others, but what it does is create an unbusinesslike impression. Use plain white typing paper for your résumé. Two pages is the maximum for a résumé. One page is even better. Don't bore your reader. Give a capsule description of your career goals and then list past experience that is in line with those goals. You may include a covering letter if you are mailing your résumé. The letter may be on distinctive stationery.

The next step after having zeroed in on your goals and written an effective résumé is the interview—the most delicate step of all in the job-hunting procedure.

How do you mitigate the stress of a job interview? Again, you can turn to your public library and read books on how to conduct yourself during the interview.

Some will give you helpful suggestions; others are filled with "tricks" and strategies. Read too many of them and your head will swim with advice, much of which will only serve to confuse. What you might keep in mind is that the interviewer is a human being just as you are. Approach him as a human being and also keep in mind that he is as eager to fill the position as you are to be the one to fill it.

Because it is his interview, let him run it. Don't you take over. On the other hand, if he opens with "Tell me about yourself," do be prepared to do just that. I don't mean for you to talk about how much you love tennis or your other favorite things. Keep your talk relevant to the matter at hand: how you can help him by what you can do in the job for which you are applying. However, don't adopt the tone of a braggart. In as even a tone as you can muster, simply state your qualifications in a positive manner.

Practice what you would say by role-playing the job interview situation with a friend. She plays "boss"; you play "applicant." Go out on every interview you can, even if you are not particularly interested in the job, and use your persuasive powers to see if you can get a job offer. The practice will sharpen your interview technique.

Do we have to tell you to bathe and clean your nails before the interview? You should be "spanking clean." Dressing as you would for the job for which you are applying will help the interviewer to better conceptualize you in that job. There are several magazines for working women that have articles and photographs of how women in the work world are dressing today. Do consult them. Avoid wearing an armload of bracelets to an interview. Their jangling is particularly annoying to male bosses, as is strong perfume. If you are in doubt about how much is too much, it is better to leave the bracelets and perfume home.

What you are doing during an interview is selling a product: You. Just as a TV commercial would not introduce negative elements about a product, don't you offer any negative information about yourself. If the interviewer asks why you left your last job, do not blame your previous employer. The interviewer might get the impression that you are a complainer or, worse, a troublemaker. However, do have some plausible answer to the question and make the answer a positive reason. No one wants to hire a "loser." Also, don't speak about how long you have been looking for work. You won't get a good job on sympathy, and again you only sound like a loser, even though you aren't.

Things are going smoothly. It looks as though you may have the job, and the question of salary comes up. The interviewer may tell you outright what the salary is. He may ask you what salary you expect—a tough question. Be prepared with a salary in mind before the interview. You should have gleaned from the Occupational Outlook Handbook, want ads in your city's newspapers, and friends in the industry what the average salary for the job is. Keep within a range of $3,000 of the average. You should have tallied your financial needs and decided that you can live fairly comfortably on the salary you are asking. In figuring salary, to be realistic, you should give weight to the fringe benefits offered. You may be willing to take a lower salary than you expected if fringe benefits—paid or low-cost medical coverage, tuition benefits, liberal expense account, company auto—make up for it.

In reply to the question "What salary do you expect?" you might ask the interviewer what the company has budgeted for the job. You don't have to be that blatant, but the answer to that question is what you want to get out of him. Anyone hiring does not interview without knowing from the department that controls the company's purse strings what the salary range is for the job.

Using the "What have you budgeted for this job?" strategy keeps you from pricing yourself out or selling yourself short financially by quoting a salary below what they expect to pay.

Your first goals in an interview should be to find out (1) what the duties of the job are and (2) what kind of person they are looking for. If you are at all perceptive, you can tell from the answers to the above whether you are or are not qualified for the job. The interviewer might tell you outright you are not right for the job. You may tell him he is mistaken and go on to tell him what you can do for him. He might have purposely told you that you are not qualified to put you on your mettle to prove to him that you are. Putting the onus on you, he wants to see if you can sell yourself.

Send the interviewer a thank-you letter after the appointment. Thank him for seeing you. Bring out points you want to reinforce that came out in the interview. Clarify other points in a positive light and perhaps bring out points there were not time for in the interview.

Let a reasonable length of time go by, say two weeks, if you have not heard from the company, before calling to see if you got the job. You can find out from the personnel source that brought you in if it is a big company. With a small company, call the interviewer himself.

If they say they have made a decision and it isn't you, you should not be afraid to ask in a polite manner, "Can you tell me why I didn't get the job?" Say you respect their decision and ask what kind of experience you would need to fill a position such as theirs. The interviewer will tell you. After that, thank him for his advice, tell him you will explore the ideas he has given you, and ask if he will consider you for another job in the future.

Looking for a job is a job in itself and should be regarded that way. It demands your full time and energy to secure a position that is not just in the "It will do" category, but one that is a stepping stone toward larger career goals.

7

How to Get
Promotions and Raises

You have done your soul searching and determined your career goals, but you find that you are in a dead-end job. How do you get out of the typing pool?

Some experts on women's careers think you should quit the company. Find a job elsewhere that fits in with your career goals and that does not label you as a typist. They suggest that you have a frank talk with your superior and let him or her know that you are not happy at your work because it is not leading to what your dream is. It does not have the responsibility or pay that you want. Give the company plenty of time to replace you. Do not leave behind ill feelings and do ask if you may use them as a job reference.

We believe that before you consider quitting a company you should speak up. When you are putting in your time in the typing pool, be as efficient and productive as you can. However, do let your immediate superior and the personnel department (if there is one) know that you are interested in a higher position. Trouble is, most women are self-effacing. They have not been taught to ask for what they want. They may feel that advancement will come only if they do a good job. The truth is that no one will promote you unless you definitely make it known that you are interested in promotion. If you have trouble speaking up, consider an assertiveness training workshop.

Large corporations post job descriptions, qualifications they are looking for, and salaries for positions on bulletin boards. Keep track of these notices. If you don't have the qualifications for the job you want, ask yourself if it is worth your while to get the training required. Could you go to school at night and get the degree that will qualify you for management?

Do keep track of extra tasks you take on in your present position. If you helped figure next year's budget, make a note of it in your career folder. If you kept an accounting of supplies, note that too. Volunteer to help people in other jobs if they seem pressured. That way you will get a feel for other work and also establish yourself as someone who can take on the added responsibility that a higher position requires. Volunteer for extra projects in the company that take you out of your department so that you may find out more about the company and how other jobs fit into its operation. Take advantage of any errands to other departments to get to know others in the company and enlarge your contacts.

If yours is a small company, opportunities are greater to do the aforementioned because there is a more informal division of labor. Let your boss know that you are interested in advancement and are working on qualifying yourself for it.

Dress for the next level to which you wish to move. Workers in the typing pool may wear jeans, but you should not. If management is your aim, wear the costume worn by management—a suit and blouse, if that is it. No one seeing you in jeans will visualize you in management, but if you are wearing a suit and blouse, you look as though you belong there.

Are you already in the position of an ascending career woman? Is your aim the upper-level management or recognition as a top professional? Cultivate your public image. Make people aware of you and your achievements through personal publicity.

How do you go about getting personal publicity? First determine what it is that you have to say. Can you offer advice about how to get ahead? Or the pitfalls of success? Or balancing a career and home responsibilities? New developments in your profession? Second, think about who would be interested: Business associates? Others in your profession? Students? The general public? Third, determine where you can best reach your audience: Through the local newspaper? A trade or professional journal? A local radio call-in show? As luncheon speaker at a business or professional organization? If your company has a public relations department, make friends there and supply them with material about yourself. If your company is too small to have one, you can be your own PR department. Find out the name of the person in charge of sections of newspapers or magazines where news about you would fit in. Supply that person with material about you and your activities. Let him or her know you are available for further information or interviewing.

When looking for publicity outlets, do not overlook your alumni association, professional societies, and community organizations that recognize achievement. Let them broadcast news about you in their publications.

A relatively new phenomenon—it has only blossomed within the past five years—is the outcropping of new women's business and professional clubs in every major city in the country. Business and professional women finding themselves excluded or made to feel uncomfortable at men's luncheon and dinner clubs are starting their own. They are networks representing a new form of female bonding of ambitious, career-minded women. Isolated business and professional women are reaching out to each other through these networks or clubs to share information and fellowship and to expand their consciousness.

Some network clubs have open membership—anyone may join. Others have strict entrance requirements—members must come from certain levels of business or be professionals, or members must be earning at least $25,000. It may be worth your while to investigate and see whether or not you are eligible to join a network to help you find your way toward your career goal.

You say you like your job, you are on your way up, but inflation is fast outstripping your salary? In other words, all you need is a raise to make things perfect for you. Before asking for an increase, find out what your company's policy is. Are there set salary ranges for each job classification? Are there specific times for salary reviews? Be prepared when asking for a raise to cite particular tasks you perform outside the strict interpretation of your job classification. Show how what you do is increasing the corporation's profits. Tell with specifics how you are worth the increase.

How will you know how much to ask for? Do a little detective work. Investigate salary ranges for similar jobs in similar industries by perusing want ads, by asking other women in your network, by asking the secretary of your trade or professional association.

When you do go to your boss to ask for a raise, be ready to negotiate. Ask for the top you hope to get, but be willing to bargain. Men do it all the time. If the idea frightens you, try the old role-playing technique with a friend beforehand. Have your friend give reasons why the company cannot give you a raise. You counter the objections with a strong defense. Imagine you are F. Lee Bailey facing a jury. Appeal to reason as well as your boss's sense of fair play. Above all, don't lose your cool and threaten to walk out. Your boss may actually take you up on that, and then where will you be? Out of a job and with poor references.

If the answer to your request is no, and you firmly believe that you are worth more, you might bide your time. What you have done is planted the notion of an increase. You have put your boss on notice that you are aiming for more. Chances are he will pay more attention to you and what you are doing for the firm and may very well rethink his position in the near future.

You have two legal aids in your career life: the Equal Pay Act and the Equal Employment Opportunity Act.

The Equal Pay Act, passed on June 10, 1963, prohibits discrimination in wages on the basis of sex for jobs that require equal skill, effort, and responsibility and that are performed under equal working conditions. Although the law applies to both men and women, women have primarily benefited because they are discriminated against in pay far more often than men. Before the act, a woman often found herself being paid less than a male co-worker for the same work. Now, thanks to the Equal Pay Act, discrimination in pay is being eliminated wherever the act applies. Men and women work in the same establishment and receive the same pay for equal work in a wide spectrum of occupations, including accounting, data processing, sales, manufacturing, and machinery repair. Vigorous enforcement of the law, coupled with favorable court decisions, is helping thousands of women.

In the first significant equal pay decision in 1970 (*Schultz* v. *Wheaton Glass*), Chief Judge Abraham L. Freedman, U.S. Third Circuit Court of Appeals, aptly described the law as "a broad charter of women's rights in the economic field" that "sought to overcome the age-old belief in women's inferiority and to eliminate the depressing effects on living standards of reduced wages for female workers and the economic and social consequences which flow from it."

In 1972 the protection of the Equal Pay Act was extended to executives, professional and administrative employees, and outside salespersons. The 1974 amendments to the Fair Labor Standards Act expanded coverage of the Equal Pay Act to large numbers of employees, including most federal, state, and local government employees (employees of state and local schools and hospitals were previously covered) as well as employees of certain small chain stores, telegraph agency employees, and employees of large motion picture theaters.

Application of the equal pay standard is not dependent on job classifications or titles, but rather on actual job requirements and performances. Minor or inconsequential differences in job content do not render the equal pay standard inapplicable. Jobs need only be substantially equal for purposes of comparison under the Equal Pay Act.

A Department of Labor publication on the subject cites this example: "The equal pay standard applies to men and women bank tellers required to perform substantially the same work, even though some of the men may be asked to perform such incidental tasks as lifting large boxes of supplies or infrequently acting as a public relations representative for the bank."

The Equal Employment Opportunity Commission enforces the Equal Pay Act. If you have a complaint

regarding equal pay, for the address of your regional
EEOC office write:

> Equal Employment Opportunity Commission
> 2401 E Street N.W.
> Washington, DC 20506

You should know, however, that in high-level or professional jobs there usually is a salary spread based on
such factors as experience, and it is very difficult to sub-
stantiate disparities within that range.

You may find that for advancement in your career,
or even to start your new career, you will need further
education. The next chapter will show how to finance it.

8

Financing Further Education

Have you thought about going back to school? Perhaps your education was interrupted many years ago because you needed to take a job or you dropped out to get married and raise a family. Perhaps you are a schoolteacher who has been excessed and is looking for a new career. Perhaps you are bored and dissatisfied with your life and are looking to education as a bridge to a more exciting future. You may want to learn skills that can be translated into work and its financial rewards. You may wish to retrain for another field or to qualify for upward mobility in your present field. Perhaps you want to go back to school simply to enrich yourself, to open yourself to new interests.

If you do go back to school, you will find that you are not alone. There are more than 850,000 American men and women over age thirty-five in college part-time and full-time; more than half of these, 53 percent, are women.

You say that you are not free to go back to school—you are married and have conflicting obligations to your husband? Look at this statistic: Of more than 450,000 women over age thirty-five enrolled in continuing education and college-degree programs, 70 percent are married. The majority of these students are in part-time programs.

If you have other obligations, you may want to return part-time or go part-time now and full-time later when your family responsibilities lessen. On the other hand, you may want to plunge right in and get your schooling over with as soon as possible by going full-time the whole way.

Perhaps the main reason why some women are hesitating about going back to school, why they have not firmed up their decision, is worry about where the money is going to come from. You must be prepared with the funds not only for tuition but also for extras such as books, transportation, and child care.

There are scholarships and grants, but these are not as plentiful as the demand for financial assistance, and usually they are only available for those who can go to school full-time, disqualifying the homemaker who has many family responsibilities or the working gal who cannot give up her full-time job and most probably is returning to school at night.

Some women dig into rainy-day funds, figuring that their college education is a worthy investment because after college they will earn money or, if already employed, earn more money through a better job. Some women take a part-time job to pay college expenses or cash in on salable talents. (One woman I know financed her way with sales of her sculpture.)

Many women opt for the community college because its fees are considerably lower than a private school's. Others go to state colleges or local junior colleges (transferring from the latter, possibly to a university, to continue their degree).

There are opportunities for cutting the time, and hence the costs, of acquiring a college education. Explore, for example, the possibilities of credit by examination. Many colleges award credit toward degrees on the basis of examinations, such as the College-Level Examination Program (CLEP) developed by the College Board or the College Proficiency Examination Program (CPEP). Colleges offering this opportunity award credit for one- or two-semester courses and grant up to two years of college credits. Inquire at several colleges about this. Not all colleges offer it, and colleges that do vary in how much credit they award.

Credit for previous learning is offered by a growing number of colleges. Credit may be given after evaluation of your work for previous courses at other schools and courses at your place of employment, for adult education courses in your local school system, or perhaps for courses taken during military service. Credit is awarded on the basis of recommendations by the American Council on Education. Life and work experience also can qualify you for credits at some colleges after evaluation by the college of the learning that occurred.

External degree programs provide the opportunity for earning an undergraduate degree by taking low-cost examinations and transferring credit for courses taken previously and/or independent study. You do not have to attend classes, and students from any state may qualify, so if you live in, say, Wyoming, you want a degree from an institution in Massachusetts, it may be possible in this way.

Nontraditional degree programs are increasingly offered by many colleges. You can study at various connected colleges and take as long as you want or need for getting the degree.

Some colleges offer courses on television, on radio, in newspapers, or through the mail. You listen to or read the lectures and write a paper or take an examination sent through the mail, and pay a relatively small amount for course credit.

There are grants and scholarships available to women, but as I said before not enough of them. However, do investigate the possibility. You may be just the woman who qualifies for one. For lists of grants and scholarships and further information about applying for them, write for the following:

Paying for Your Education: A Guide for Adult Learners
College Board Publications Orders
Box 2815
Princeton, NJ 08541

General Information for the Returning Student
Catalyst
14 East 60th Street
New York, NY 10022

An excellent book on the topic is *A Woman's Guide to Career Preparation: Scholarships, Grants & Loans* by Ann J. Jawin (New York: Anchor, Doubleday, 1979). (Because costs vary from place to place and time to time, I have not included prices, but they are modest.)

If you work for a large or medium-size corporation, there is a good chance that your company will pay for at least part of your schooling. A poll of 614 firms taken by the National Industrial Conference Board a few years ago found that 89 percent offered some kind of tuition refund program. Usually a company will pay from half to all of the tuition costs for courses related to a full-time employee's current job or possible advancement within the company. In addition, some will reimburse the fees for books and other expenses, even for classes that are not related to the job, as long as an employee's studies do not interfere with her work.

One young woman we know who was employed by a large New York City department store as a floor manager went back to school to take her master's degree in business administration, majoring in retailing. The store paid a large chunk of her tuition and, impressed with her ambition, promoted her to assisant merchandise manager for several departments. Furthermore, because her M.B.A. was undertaken to enhance her skills in her job, she was allowed by Internal Revenue to deduct from her individual tax return the part of the tuition she had to pay.

Work-study programs are a good way to get an education, learn a job, and get paid for it, too. Some companies offer programs in which periods of study alternate with periods of paid on-the-job training. Companies that do this include:

Allied Chemical Corporation
Box 2245-R
Morristown, NJ 07960

Kentucky Carbon Corporation
One Valley Square
Charleston, WV 25301

U.S. Steel Corporation
600 Grant Street
Pittsburgh, PA 15221

Over 900 U.S. colleges and universities offer work-study programs in a variety of fields. You have the opportunity of learning on the job and earning money to help with college costs, too. Two colleges that have outstanding work-study programs are Antioch College, Yellow Springs, Ohio; and Northeastern University, Boston, Massachusetts.

Do not overlook your business or professional organization, which may very well have grants, scholarships, or interest-free or low-cost loans available to those in their field or interested in entering their field. Your local Chamber of Commerce should not be overlooked either for the same.

The largest single source of financial aid is the U.S. government. There are five federal student aid programs. To qualify for aid you must meet the following conditions:

1. You must be planning to study at least half-time. That is a minimum of six credits per semester.
2. You must be enrolled or planning to enroll in a program that leads to a degree or certificate.
3. You must be planning to attend an eligible program at one of the 4,500 colleges, universities, vocational schools, or hospital schools of nursing, or to participate in an approved external degree program that is approved to offer financial aid.
4. You must sign and have notarized an affidavit stating that you will use the money only for tuition, fees, room, board, books, supplies, and other items related to your attendance at a particular school and that the money is not going to be used for noneducational purposes.

The federal government's Basic Educational Opportunity Grant Program (BEOG) makes funds available to eligible students attending approved colleges, community/junior colleges, vocational schools, technical institutes, hospital schools of nursing, and other post–high school institutions. Unlike loans, these grants do not have to be paid back. You can apply for a basic grant by completing one of several different forms. You should contact the financial aid office at the school(s) you are considering to determine which form to use. The forms are available at high schools and post–high school institutions. You should hear four to six weeks from filing whether you are eligible for a grant. The only sure way to find out if you are eligible is by applying. The grants are normally based on your income for the previous year (the year you apply). If unemployment, disability, separation, divorce, or death of a working spouse has reduced your current family income since you submitted your first application, you should file a supplemental form obtained from the financial aid office of the school(s) you are applying to. The alteration in your income may very well mean that you now qualify for a grant.

How much do grants give? Awards range from $200 to $1,800.

If you receive notice that you are eligible, submit the notification to your school, which will calculate the amount of the basic grant you are eligible to receive. You may submit the notification to more than one school. The amount of your award will be based on determination of your eligibility and the cost of attending your school.

National Direct Student Loans (NDSL) are for students who are enrolled at least half-time at a participating postsecondary institution and who need a loan to meet their educational expenses.

You may borrow up to a total of (a) $2,500 if you are enrolled in a vocational program or if you have completed less than two years of a program leading to a bachelor's degree; (b) $5,000 if you are an undergraduate student who has already completed two years of study toward a bachelor's degree (this total includes any amount you borrowed for your first two years of study under this program); (c) $10,000 for graduate or professional study. This total includes any amount you borrowed under this program for your undergraduate study.

Repayment begins nine months after you graduate or leave school for other reasons. You may be allowed up to ten years to pay back the loan. During the repayment period you are charged 3 percent interest on the unpaid balance of the loan principal. The amount of your payment depends upon the size of your debt, but usually you must pay at least $30 per month. If the school agrees to a lesser amount, it may be due to extraordinary circumstances, such as prolonged unemployment.

Apply through the financial aid officer at your school. He can also tell you about loan cancellation provisions for borrowers who go into certain fields of teaching or specified military duty.

Supplemental Educational Opportunity Grants (SEOG) are a gift of money for students with exceptional financial need who without the grant would be unable to continue their education. Graduate students are not eligible for these grants.

If you receive one of these grants, it cannot be less than $200 or more than $1,500 a year. Normally, the grant may be received for four years. However, the grant may be received for five years when the course of study requires the extra time. The total that may be awarded is $4,000 for a four-year course of study or $5,000 for a five-year course.

If you are selected for one of these grants, your educational institution must provide you with additional financial assistance at least equal to the amount of the grant.

Apply through your financial aid officer. He is responsible for determining who will receive one of these grants and the amount.

The College Work-Study (CWS) Program provides jobs for students who have great financial need and who must earn a part of their educational expenses. You may apply if you are enrolled at least half-time as a graduate, undergraduate, or vocational student in an approved postsecondary educational institution.

The educational institution that participates in College Work-Study arranges jobs on or off campus with a public or private nonprofit agency such as a hospital. If you are found to be eligible, you may be employed for as many as forty hours a week.

In arranging a job and determining how many hours a week you may work under the program, the financial aid officer will take into account your need for financial assistance, your class schedule, and your health and academic progress. In general, the salary you receive is is at least equal to the current minimum wage. The maximum hourly wage rate depends on the job and your qualification.

Apply through the financial aid officer of your school. He is responsible for determining your eligibility and arranging the job.

The Guaranteed Student Loan (GSL) Program enables students to borrow directly from lenders in order to finance educational expenses. While the bulk of these loans are made by commercial lenders (banks, credit unions, savings and loan institutions), some states and educational institutions are also lenders. The loans are insured by the federal government or guaranteed by a state or private nonprofit guarantee agency.

You may apply for one of these loans if you are

already enrolled in good standing and making satisfactory progress or have been accepted for enrollment at least half-time in an eligible college, university, or professional school or an eligible vocational, technical, trade, business, or home-study school.

The maximum you may borrow as an undergraduate is $2,500 per academic year. Graduate and professional students may borrow up to $5,000 per academic year. (In some states the maximums are less.) The total you may borrow for undergraduate or vocational study is $7,500. The total for graduate and professional students is $15,000, including any amount borrowed for undergraduate study.

Loan payments begin between nine and twelve months after you leave school. The lender generally must allow you at least five years to repay the loan and may allow up to ten years. When you leave school, you must contact your lender to establish a repayment schedule. The amount of your payments depends upon the size of your debt. You should ask your lender what your monthly payments will be before you take out the loan.

Important: In contrast to the other U.S. Office of Education programs, your eligibility for a GSL is not based on your family's financial status. This is of benefit to women who do not qualify for other programs because possibly their husbands' incomes are too high, thus disqualifying them for aid.

A Health Education Assistance Loan (HEAL) is a federal insured loan made to full-time students pursuing one of the following degrees at a school that takes part in the HEAL program:

Doctor of Medicine
Doctor of Osteopathy
Doctor of Dentistry

Doctor of Veterinary Medicine
Doctor of Optometry
Doctor of Podiatry
Graduate or equivalent degree in Public Health
Bachelor or master of science in Pharmacy

You can borrow up to $10,000 per academic year to a total of $50,000. Pharmacy students are limited to $7,500 per academic year to a total of $37,500.

You can get an application from the financial aid administrator at a health professions school that takes part in the HEAL program. After completing the borrower's section, you must have the financial aid administrator at your school complete the school section of the application. He or she can also refer you to a lender that takes part in the HEAL program.

Loan payments begin nine months afer you either complete formal training, including accredited internship and residency periods, or cease to be a full-time student at a HEAL school. Interest is payable while you are in school. However, at the option of your lender, interest may accrue and be compounded no more frequently than semiannually while you are in school or during the grace period and periods of internship, residency, and authorized deferments.

You are generally allowed from ten to fifteen years to repay the loan. When you leave school you must contact your lender to establish a repayment schedule. The amount of your payments depends upon the size of your debt. The interest rate on the HEAL loan may not exceed 12 percent (annual percentage rate) on the unpaid balance. There is no federal interest subsidy on a HEAL loan. This means that you must pay the interest on the loan while you are attending school.

From education loans, we skip in the next chapter to credit, an important aspect of money management.

9

Credit

Why should you have credit cards and charge accounts? Why not continue to pay cash for everything you buy? Isn't it easier to keep track of your budget that way? Maybe so, but look at these cases:

You are window shopping and you spot a dress that would be perfect to wear to your sister's wedding. The price is right. Trouble is, it's two more weeks to payday and you are short of cash. If you had a charge card with that store, you could have that dress in time for the wedding.

You are up to your ears in household chores and you hear that your best friend is in the hospital. You don't really have time to spare to run to the florist. If you had a charge account there, you could telephone your order.

It's income tax time. You know that you entertained prospective buyers for your line of handcrafted jewelry, but you can't remember where and when and how much you spent. If you had charged those entertainments to a credit card, you would have had an automatic record of expenditures for a business entertainment deduction.

The advantages of credit cards and charges are:

1. You don't have to carry a great deal of cash with you.

2. They facilitate financial record keeping.
3. You can shop by telephone. It is easier to shop by mail.
4. You can buy bargains when you are short of cash.
5. You are covered for emergencies at home or away from home.
6. It is easier to make returns.

On the other hand, you should know that there are disadvantages to charging. If you cannot meet your monthly statement, there is usually an interest charge of 1.5 percent on the unpaid balance or 18 percent per year. If you charge more to the card with an unpaid balance, you may be charged interest on the new purchases from the day you bought them. And disadvantage number two comes in here: It is very easy to regard that plastic card as an "open sesame" to spending for any items that catch your eye. You may become a "charge-a-holic," forgetting that those purchases must be paid for with hard-earned money. Department stores do encourage charge cards because they know that charge cards in turn encourage impulse buying.

However, you may be a well-disciplined person who can handle credit. How do you go about getting it? You should have a checking account and at least one savings account. The checking account should not have a record of being overdrawn and you should have enough in your savings account so that the store is convinced that you can cover purchases. Your credit application will ask for the name of your employer or, if you are self-employed, the name of your business. It will ask how long you have been employed at your present job or how long you have been in business for yourself and your yearly salary. It will ask how long you have lived at your present address and at your previous address. It will ask for number of dependents and for you to list bank references where you have accounts.

Once you have filled out and returned a credit application, you have begun a credit record with a credit bureau computer. There are five major credit bureaus in the United States, and they sell their services based on the information in their computers to help their clients decide whether or not to grant you credit.

The credit bureau or store will check to see if you are employed where you say you are, for how long, and what your title is. They will check with your banks to see that your checking account is not overdrawn and that you do have a savings account where you say you do. If you have a previous credit record, your store will want to know if your payment record has been satisfactory for the last three to five years.

Warning: Don't lie on your credit application. That will get you an automatic turn-down.

The Fair Credit Reporting Act of 1971 forbids credit bureaus or stores to question your neighbors or friends about your morals or character.

The Equal Credit Opportunity Act of 1974 prohibits discrimination in the extension of credit based on sex or marital status. In 1976 it was amended to prohibit, in addition, discrimination based on race, color, religion, age, national origin, and receipt of public assistance (welfare). It is illegal now for creditors to deny credit because your income is derived from part-time employment or from a pension, annuity, or retirement benefit program. Furthermore, creditors must consider consistently received alimony, child support, or separate maintenance payments as income, although they do have the right to ask for proof that this part of your income is consistently received.

The federal Credit Opportunity Act also states that you have the right to have credit in your maiden name

(Mary Smith), your first name and your husband's surname (Mary Jones), or your first name and a combined surname (Mary Smith-Jones). You have the right to get credit without a co-signer if you meet the creditor's standards and the right to keep your own accounts after you change your name or marital status or reach a certain age or retire (unless the creditor has evidence that you are unable or unwilling to repay).

Types of credit fall into several categories. There are the personal charge accounts at small local stores, such as the little dress shop or the hardware store. These stores issue no charge card. They usually bill by hand once a month. Often they don't add interest charges if you are late with payment. Large department stores such as Saks Fifth Avenue, B. Altman's, and Bloomingdale's have their own charge cards. Bills are on computer and you are billed once a month. You may use the same charge card at any of the branches. A department store may have two basic types of accounts: one charging no interest but requiring payment at the end of the month, and the other a revolving account where you pay installments and owe interest on the unpaid balance.

Oil companies, airlines, car rental companies, and telephone companies have charge cards, too. Most charge interest for late payments.

The aforementioned are all single-purpose cards. They may only be used for charges to the specific company that has issued the card.

Multipurpose cards, bank credit cards such as BankAmerica, Master Card, and Visa, are accepted by many shops and services throughout the United States. If you have a good credit rating, you may secure the card without cost. However, increasingly, bank credit cards are charging a fee for the card, and government is pressuring for this change. Bank credit card companies usually charge 1½ percent interest or 18 percent annual interest on late charges. This is how they make their money, so they are not touchy about late payment as long as you eventually pay.

Travel and entertainment cards such as American Express, Diners' Club, and Carte Blanche charge an annual fee for use of the card. They receive a percentage for their services from the hotels, restaurants, and other companies who accept their card. They expect prompt payment. If you fall behind, there may be a late charge and you risk not being able to renew your card when your year is up.

Once you have a credit card and have established a record of prompt payment, you will have no trouble probably getting other credit cards. But what if you don't have a credit card? How do you get that first one?

You might take out a small loan that you do not really need at your bank. Pay it back promptly. You have established yourself as a good credit risk. Or you might do what Mary Louise K. did. She went to the bank where her firm does business, accompanied by her boss, who vouched for the fact that she was of good character and a good credit risk. The manager of the bank branch was delighted to issue Mary Louise his bank's charge card, and she did not have to go to the trouble of taking out a loan or paying interest to establish her credit.

If you are married and wish to establish your own line of credit, make sure that the name on your credit card takes the form of, say, Mary Smith rather than Mrs. John Smith, so that your rather than your husband's credit is established with prompt payments. Look over your credit cards. If they are made out to your husband's first name and surname, call or write and ask that your creditor send a form so that you can change their status. The creditor must agree, according to the Equal Opportunity Credit Law, as long as payments are continued to be made. This step will ensure that you have a credit rating in case you are widowed or divorced.

As a matter of fact, if you marry, divorce, separate, or are widowed, you should make a special point to call or visit your local credit bureau (see the Yellow Pages for location and telephone number) to make sure that all relevant information normally carried by the credit bureau is in a credit file under your own name.

Consider the case of Peggy L., who had been divorced for one year. She wanted to get credit in her own name, but had difficulty. A department store contacted her because her former husband was delinquent on credit card charges incurred when they were married. Peggy agreed to pay the charges herself and reapplied to have the credit card reissued in her name. She was turned down because of the delinquent payments. She wrote back, explaining that she had made good on the payments. Peggy investigated and found that the delinquent account was a joint account and therefore became part of her credit history. Since she did not notify the creditor at the time of her divorce and accepted responsibility for the account after the divorce, she was not able to get the unfavorable information removed. She decided to ask the credit bureau to include in her file an explanation of what happened. She also contacted the regional credit manager of the department store, asking him to reconsider her application in light of the explanation of the circumstances. She stressed her voluntary commitment to pay the delinquent account and showed proof of payment. She received her new credit card.

Take the case of Gloria G., who was widowed in her sixties. Gloria had had a few department store credit cards in her own name when her husband was living. At the time her husband had been dead six months, she wanted to apply for a travel and entertainment card. She had no employment record of her own, though her husband had been a substantial businessman and had paid all bills promptly. Gloria's income now came from Social Security payments and dividends on stock left her by her husband and from insurance proceeds. Because she was not employed, she wondered whether she could obtain the credit card. She learned that the Equal Credit Opportunity Act entitled her to count social security, dividends, and insurance proceeds as income, and because they totaled to a substantial amount, she was credit-worthy. She received her card.

What should you do if you are denied credit? (I presume, of course, that you have sufficient income and a good financial record. If these were lacking in the case of a man, he would be turned down for credit, too.) The Equal Credit Opportunity Act says you have the right to know within thirty days of filing it whether your application was accepted or rejected. If your application was rejected, you have the right to know why. The creditor must either immediately give you the specific reason(s) for the rejection or tell you that you have the right to specific reasons if you made a request within sixty days. Examples of specific reasons are "Your income was too low" or "You haven't been employed at your job long enough." Indefinite and vague reasons such as "You didn't meet our minimum standards" or "You didn't receive enough points on our credit scoring system" do not comply with the law.

Let the creditor know that you are aware of the Equal Credit Opportunity Act and that he is violating that act.

You can also sue the creditor. You have the right to bring a case in a federal district court. If you win, you can recover your actual damages and punitive damages of up to $10,000. You can also recover reasonable attorney's fees and court costs. A private attorney can advise you on how to proceed.

If you join up with other people and file a class action suit, you may recover punitive damages for the class of up to $500,000 or 1 percent of the creditor's net worth, whichever is less.

You can report violations against you of the Equal Credit Opportunity Act to the Federal Trade Commission, Washington, DC 20580, or to its regional office as listed in the phone book. This helps the commission in enforcing the law, though they cannot handle your private case. Many states also have equal credit opportunity laws of their own. Check with your state's attorney general.

If the grantor tells you that you were denied credit because of an adverse credit report, the federal Credit Reporting Act of 1971 mandates that he must give you the name and address of the credit bureau he used. Go to the bureau in person with identification or make a written request that you be given the information by telephone. If you go or write within thirty days of being denied credit, you can review your file at no charge. The reason for the written request, or identification if you visit personally, is to protect your privacy so that no one else may gain access to your credit file. You are entitled, though, to take anyone with you to the credit bureau to help you check your file. Here is what the credit bureau must do:

1. The credit bureau must tell you the names of everyone who received a report on you within the preceding six months, or within the preceding two years if the report was furnished for employment purposes.

2. It must reinvestigate incomplete or incorrect information. If the information is incorrect or cannot be

verified, the bureau must remove it from your file. (There is always the possibility that your file got mixed up with someone else's, especially if your name was changed because of marriage or divorce.)

3. It must, if it is in error, notify creditors who received your file during the past six months that an error was made. This must be done free of charge to you. You might even request that they send corrected files to people who inquired about your credit standing even longer ago than six months.

4. It must, if there is a disagreement between you and the bureau about information in your file, put your version of the story in a statement of 100 words in your file and include it in all future reports to would-be creditors. A case might be that you have refused to pay a creditor because merchandise arrived broken and was not replaced. You have been listed as a bad payer with that creditor, but at least future creditors will read your argument and perhaps overlook lack of payment to that creditor.

5. It must not report adverse information about you after seven years or bankruptcy information for fourteen years.

Perhaps you went haywire and forgot that your plastic cards must be backed with money. We suggest that you not charge anything unless you have the money to pay for it or can be absolutely certain that the money is coming in within a short time. If you have accumulated a pile of bills and fallen delinquent and have been doing this consistently, you will get a bad credit rating. How do you go straight? Decide that you are going to resist temptation. Hide your credit cards. If need be, cut them in half and throw them in the wastebasket. Do not charge anything for one year. Pay off every single one of your bills. If you owe just one store, no other creditors will extend credit. Then take an installment loan for something you need, say, an appliance or auto, so that the lender might accept you because he has the security of repossessing if you fail to meet payments. However, you must be very certain to meet payments on time. You might have to go to a finance company rather than a bank because they are more liberal in extending credit, though they do charge higher interest rates. After about a year or so of prompt payments, you might apply to a department store for credit. Caution: If you are accepted for a charge card, you must realize that the store is taking a chance on you and will watch your payment record very carefully!

Now that you know a great deal about the ins and outs of credit and have your credit cards, guard them carefully. They are equal to money. Many are the horror stories of stolen credit cards. Never leave your cards in an unguarded situation. Always make sure after making a purchase that the salesperson gives you back your card. Many fraudulent charges are made by store employees who "forget" to give you back your charge card. Cut your old cards in half before throwing them in the wastebasket. Always sign a new card as soon as you get it. Keep a list of credit cards, their numbers, and the addresses and phone numbers of the stores that issued them with your financial records.

If your card is stolen, call your card issuers promptly. You are not responsible for any charges after you have notified them. Follow up your call with a letter, stating that you called on a certain day at a certain time and to whom you spoke. If you don't report the loss of a card, you are responsible for up to $50 of fraudulent charges on *each* card.

Our next chapter discusses more about credit and about loans.

10

Loans

"Neither a borrower nor a lender be," that oft-quoted admonition by Shakespeare's Polonius, is not always the best advice. Let's take the borrowing first. There are times when debt can be a positive thing. We call it "planned" debt. You are borrowing for a positive purpose and you are confident of your ability to meet payment terms.

You are a sales manager for a large department store. You are offered the position of general manager of a suburban branch at a higher salary. The catch is, you need a car to commute and you don't have one. Borrowing to buy a car in this case is planned debt.

You have your teeth capped to enhance your smile. The dental bill is large, but if you pay it before December 31, you get a medical tax deduction. You borrow to finish payments and garner deduction. Planned debt.

Your utility bills are zooming out of sight. New insulation and replacing an old hot-water heater would bring those bills down (you would also be entitled to an energy credit on your tax return). You borrow to pay for new insulation and a new hot-water heater. Again, planned debt.

When is it right to borrow?

1. To buy big-ticket items such as a car, appliances that are needed but that would deplete your cash reserve if purchased for cash
2. For emergencies—valid ones
3. To finance education for yourself, your spouse, or your children
4. To buy a home, cooperative, or condominium because you will have gained equity in return
5. To go into business, but only after you have thoroughly researched the solidity of your venture
6. To finance investments that will bring a sure return

When is it *wrong* to borrow?

1. When you can't repay, but simply can't resist buying an item
2. When it depletes your cash reserve (which should be two to three months' salary)
3. When borrowing is for a risky venture
4. When you are borrowing to meet everyday expenses because you are living above your means

Say you plan to take out a loan for one of the right reasons. How much debt can you safely take on? Most experts would say that you probably can handle a loan of up to 20 percent of your after-tax income. Beyond that is putting the squeeze on yourself.

Okay, so you have a right reason for borrowing and you plan not to exceed that 20 percent. What kind of loan can you get? There are a number, each with its advantages and disadvantages.

Unsecured Personal Loan. This is the loan for which you do not put up collateral. It is extended on the basis of your character, previous credit history, and regularity of income. You do sign a loan agreement that entitles the lender to certain recourses as outlined in the agreement if you default on the loan: (For example, a bank may seize your savings account.) Interest is higher on an unsecured loan where there is no collateral.

Secured Personal Loan. This is the loan that is secured with collateral. Collateral may be anything that your borrower might accept. Of course, it is usually something of substantial value—a car, stocks, bonds, jewelry. Often the borrower will hold the collateral until the loan is fully paid up. Usually interest is lower on a secured loan, and you may be able to borrow a larger amount.

Passbook Loans. You may borrow against your savings account at the bank where you deposit. Your passbook is their collateral. You borrow at a rate of a few percentage points above your interest. Usually the bank will lend you up to 90 percent of what is in your account. You could also simply withdraw the money from the bank and avoid paying interest altogether, but if you think you may have trouble replacing the money in your savings account that you have "loaned" to yourself, it is better to take a passbook loan.

Life Insurance Policy Loan. This is a low-cost loan. The percentage of interest is lower than most other types of loans. However, keep in mind that you are borrowing against the cash value of your policy and that if you die before the loan is returned, your insurance coverage is reduced by the value of the loan.

Auto Loans. These may be secured from your auto dealer as well as from a bank or credit union. Auto dealer loans are almost always much higher than the others on interest. Usually you finance a car for two years and pay in monthly installments. You can get a longer-life loan, but the longer the life of the loan, the higher the interest.

Home Mortgage, Condominium, and Cooperative Apartment Loans. The security for these, of course, is your living quarters. As of the writing of this book, interest rates are very high, so you will wind up paying more than twice the price of your home. However, the more you can put down as down payment on the mortgage, the less interest you will have to pay.

Education Loans. If you qualify, the government secures student loans for the bank where you apply for the loan. Interest begins with the taking out of the loan, but you have up to ten years to repay the loan. Interest at 7 percent is cheaper than you can get for any other type of educational loan.

In listing types of loans, I have told you some of the places where you can go for loans. At the risk of repeating myself, I would like to list them again with other loan sources.

Credit Unions. If you can join one, do so. You will be borrowing your own money and that of your friends. Interest rates are lower than average. There is usually no charge to write your loan, and you may pay off your loan ahead of schedule without penalty. Furthermore, you pay interest only for the time the money is used. There is usually a certain length of time you must have been a member to get a loan, and you must have a certain percentage of the loan amount requested on deposit in its share account and show a good steady employment record or alternate income source.

Banks. In these days of tight money, it is a good idea to approach a bank where you are already doing business if you seek a loan. Savings banks and savings and loan institutions specialize in mortgages. Commercial banks make loans for all kinds of purposes. Rates vary among banks. Shop around for a bank with the lowest interest rates, and don't be afraid to tell your banker, if his interest rates are higher, that you can get a loan cheaper at another bank. He might just lower the rate for you in order not to lose your business.

Finance Companies. These charge higher rates than banks, usually as high as state laws allow. They will lend smaller amounts than banks, and they are not so fussy about whom they lend money to.

Overdraft Checking. The bank where you have your checking account will give you a line of credit based on your income and net worth. You then may write a check or checks for more money than you have in your account. On your bank statement you will be charged a finance charge of 1 to 1½ percent per month for the amount of credit used.

The disadvantage: If you are not well disciplined, if you are weak about money, you may find it so easy to borrow that you will be in constant debt!

Bank Credit Cards. Bank credit cards such as Master Card and Visa will also extend a line of credit to you; the amount is based on your ability to pay. Interest is also 1 to 1½ percent per month with sometimes an initial charge for the loan.

Life Insurance. As mentioned before, you are borrowing at low interest, but against the cash value of your policy, which is reduced if you die and have not paid back the loan.

Family and Friends. Family members and friends may lend money at no interest or at a lower rate than anywhere else out of love and concern for you. However, in order to avoid hard feelings that may occur, it is best to have an agreement, preferably written, on how and when you will pay back.

Your Employer. You may ask for a salary advance from your employer. We do not recommend this source for a loan. A salary advance will leave you short the following month(s) and also may cast doubt on your ability to handle money or your sense of responsibility. Better to go to a bank or finance company.

Small Business Administration. This will lend money to those starting up or expanding a business who may have been denied loans elsewhere. The federal agency has targeted $100 million for business loans to women because of previous discrimination against loans to women for going into or expanding businesses. Contact the nearest SBA office (listed under "U.S. Government" in the phone book) for further information.

Two sources for loans definitely *not* recommended are pawnbrokers and loan sharks. Pawnbrokers ask for collateral and will only give you a loan for partial value of it and at astronomical rates. You must redeem your collateral within thirty or sixty days or it becomes the property of the pawnbroker, who will sell it. If you deal with loan sharks, you are dealing with the underworld. Interest rates are 100 percent and up! Not paying back on schedule may mean their breaking both your legs!

What is it that creditors look for before they lend money? Well, they cannot take into consideration your race, color, age, sex, or marital status nor your birth-control methods. That is illegal according to the Equal Credit Opportunity Act, remember? What they do look for is how you stack up against what they call "the three C's," capacity, character, and collateral.

Capacity. Can you repay the debt? Creditors ask for employment information. What is your occupation? Is it in an unsteady field such as acting, or are you employed in a depressed industry? How long have you been working for your present employer? What is your position? How much do you earn? What are your expenses? How many dependents do you have? How much other debt are you carrying?

Character. Will you repay the debt? Creditors will take a long, hard look at your credit history. How reliable have you been in paying past debts? Do you pay bills on time? How much other debt do you have? Do you live within your means? Have you ever defaulted on a loan? (This is something that creditors frown upon, although if the default was sometime in the past and you have reestablished yourself as a good credit risk, there may be hope.) Have you, if this is a large loan, ever taken out, say, a mortgage before, or a car loan, and how was your record on that? Creditors also look for signs of stability: how long you've lived at your present address, whether you own or rent, and whether you are insured.

Collateral. Is the creditor fully protected if you fail to repay? What do you have of value that might be used to secure your loan—home, car, stocks, bonds, jewelry, paintings? What sources do you have for repaying debt other than income, such as savings, investments, or property?

Creditors give different weight to each of these "three C's." Some creditors are stricter in some categories than others. Some creditors actually have number point rating systems for each of the questions asked above. Different creditors may reach different conclusions about your credit worthiness based on the very same facts. One creditor may say "nix,"while another gives the go-ahead. If you are turned down by one financial institution, you need not necessarily give up hope. Try others.

You might find yourself on the other side of credit as a lender. You are one, of course, when you buy a government or corporate bond, but let's talk about loans to family or friends.

You have a favorite niece or nephew, an earnest and ambitious student who has decided to become a doctor.

Medical school costs are steep. You feel he/she is deserving and you want to help out by loaning money to him/her at little or no interest.

Your son and daughter-in-law would like to buy a house. You would like to see their child, your grandchild, with his own backyard in which to play. You offer to lend part of the down payment on a little ranch house.

A friend has an idea for opening a little shop featuring handmade ceramics. She asks if you could lend her money for starting-up expenses. You believe in her project and you have reserve cash.

In all of these cases and in any case where you are lending money on a personal basis, you should have a written legal agreement between you and the borrower —not only because a written legal agreement will prevent misunderstandings, but also because, if your borrower should meet with sudden death, you will have proof of a claim against his estate. Besides the written agreement, you should ask that an insurance policy be assigned to you in an amount to cover the size of the loan.

As for interest you would charge family or friends (and remember, if you don't charge interest, you are losing what you might have gained with the money in investing or in the bank), you might base it on what the going rate is at your neighborhood bank. You don't want to make it an unreasonable rate, but on the other hand, you don't want to gain the reputation of being an "easy mark."

A friend or relative might ask you to co-endorse a loan with him. You should know that your signature as a co-endorser makes you responsible for the loan, too. If the one who takes out the loan does not meet a payment, you are responsible for making that payment. If you do not, your credit line will be destroyed! Better to lend the money yourself to a friend or relative than to co-endorse a note. Then you do not run the risk of damaging your credit rating.

The next chapter tells about investing extra money.

11

Investments

Why should women be interested in knowing about investing? Well, most men are. They know that money is meant to work for them. You have gotten a handle on calculating what you are worth and know exactly what you made last year and what you spent. Now, to be a good money manager, you must know how to invest.

But doesn't investment mean risk? Yes, there is a certain amount of risk with every investment, but look at things this way: If you have all your surplus money in a daily savings account, you are really losing money. At 5¼ to 5½ percent interest, you are not even preserving your capital during these inflationary days. As a matter of fact, instead of earning money, you are actually losing it. And on top of that, you are paying income tax on the bank interest.

We are not saying you should not have a savings account at all. Before going into investments, you should have from two to three months' salary in liquid reserve for emergencies. It should be kept in the highest-yield account available. You should also have adequate life insurance (see Chapter 14). Then the money not needed for ordinary living expenses can be used for investing. Because life styles vary, we can't put a percentage figure on that amount. What one person considers a necessity for ordinary living may be considered an unnecessary luxury by another.

However, most of us have goals or dreams of what we would like for the future. It may be a vacation home, a college education for a child, a European tour, or enough funds for a comfortable retirement. Whatever that goal is, chances are that it will cost a great deal of money, and it is certain that with inflation very much in the picture for the future as well as today, you will not be able to amass the goal money via traditional savings, as you could when the rate of inflation was low and savings accounts could provide a rate of return that was higher than the inflation rate.

Consider this example. You or you and your spouse are in the 30 percent bracket with a 6 percent inflation rate. You are currently receiving a 5¼ percent interest rate from your savings account. Your real return on your money is a negative figure. If you put $10,000 in a savings account at the beginning of the year at 5¼ percent, by the end of the year the real purchasing power of your money will be only $9,746. And after five years the real purchasing power will have declined to $8,900. And if you have savings or time certificates yielding 7½ percent, after paying 30 percent in taxes and adjusting for 6 percent inflation, you would be losing 1.12 percent annually. Now you see why you must invest your money for a higher return than savings generate to make those goals of yours come true!

What do we need for a return on our capital to keep up with inflation? One vice-president of an investment firm I spoke with said, definitely: "The net return (that is, before taxes and excluding commissions) you should be looking for is 15 percent." He gave an example: You buy 100 shares of stock at $10 a share. The stock pays a 10 percent dividend. At the end of the year, say, there has been no depreciation or appreciation. You have made 10 percent. If you buy the stock at $10 and sell at $10.50, you have increased your capital by 5 percent and you have been given 10 percent income. The combined income and that capital appreciation equal 15 percent.

That 15 percent, he told me, is the dead minimum for any new investment in the stock market. By and large, he thought that one should be able to exceed that percentage over a period of time, thus continuing to outpace inflation.

How to find the right stockbroker who is right for you is covered in Chapter 23. Once you have found one, he will fill out a company form on you.

By law he must contact your bank(s) by phone or mail to verify your credit worthiness and to make sure that you are not using a fictitious name or Social Security number. Also, the new account form must be signed by your account executive, the branch manager, and a voting officer of the firm to verify the appropriateness of your investment objectives. It is to prevent the inappropriateness, for example, of a seventy-year-old woman in a nursing home playing the highly speculative commodities market. (Unfortunately, this has happened in the past. The SEC is currently prosecuting several cases with similar circumstances.)

Depending on the account executive and you, the broker might want to get more information, such as:

- What likelihood is there for increased earnings on your job?
- What is the possibility of your marrying, if you are not already married, and how will that affect your financial outlook? (For instance: Will you want your investments held jointly?)

- Are you speculatively inclined, concerned about increasing your current income, in a high tax bracket looking for tax-sheltered investments?

On the basis of information he receives from you, your broker may be in a position to set up an investment program to help you reach your financial goals.

The accompanying chart presents investment objectives and, under them, instruments of investing that will help you reach your financial objectives. Many of the terms will sound unfamiliar to you. We will spend the rest of this chapter atempting to explain in simple language what these terms mean.

Stocks are shares in the ownership of a company. If you own stock in a certain corporation, you are one of the owners of the corporation. When the corporation prospers, you share in that prosperity through increases in the price of its stock and through increased dividends. On the other hand, if your company is not doing well, the price of your stock will frequently decline, and if yours is common stock, dividends may be cut or omitted altogether.

Preferred stockholders, unlike common stockholders, are guaranteed a dividend of a certain specified amount. They must be paid before common stockholders get anything. If corporation business were so bad that it could not afford to pay its preferred stockholders their dividend, it would have to make up that amount in later years, and that cumulative amount would have to be paid before anything went to the common stockholders.

A disadvantage to preferred stock, though, is that if profits soar, its dividend percentage still remains the same and its stockholders would not receive any more money. However, the common stockholders who do not have the fixed percentage would get more.

Some stock is sold "over the counter" through special dealers rather than on the New York Stock Exchange or the American Stock Exchange or one of the regional stock exchanges. These over-the-counter shares trade between brokerage firms on clients' behalf. They are issued usually by smaller, lesser-known companies. They can offer substantial capital gains when sold if enthusiasm for the stock is high. Conversely, if there is little interest in the stock, it can be very difficult to sell or find a ready buyer. Because they involve above-average risk for making above-average profits, they are reserved for speculation. Never risk money on them that you can't afford to lose.

Selling short is also for those who can take large risks. They believe that a certain stock is going to drop. They sell the shares at a current market price, then borrow stock from their broker, putting up a part of the cost of the stock as collateral. When the stock drops, they buy the stock on the open market and use it to replace the stock they borrowed. If the stock rises, however, the investor has lost money. This process can only be entered into if the client has a preexisting margin account.

When is it best for the ordinary investor to buy stocks? There are certain historical criteria for buying:

1. Where is the stock in relation to its trading range for the year? If you are buying, you would want to buy when the stock is on the low end (conversely, when you are selling, you normally want to sell when stock is on its high end).
2. Look at the price-earnings multiple. In other words, look at how much the stock is earning in relation to its price. At how many times earning is it trading compared with others in the same industry? Looking for the lowest price

in comparison to earnings usually provides the best value.

3. Look at dividend coverage. That means how much the company is earning in relation to how much it is paying out. You would want a healthy earnings figure in relation to the dividend to ensure that dividends would continue to be paid.

4. Look at the management of the company. How solid is its operating history? What is its background? What is its track record? Is it involved in any legal problems (trouble!)? How does it treat its accounting of earnings—conservatively or aggressively?

5. What is the industry outlook for that company?

6. What is the institutional interest? Are pension funds and banks interested in the stock?

7. Research sponsorship. Are brokerage houses recommending it to their customers?

It is much more difficult to determine when it is time to sell a stock. Some people invest by a fixed percentage up or down. If their stock goes down, say, 10 percent, they sell. On the up side, they sell at 50 to 100 percent. Some people would agree about that philosophy for the down side but have a different one for the up side. For instance, if they had 200 shares at $10 (investment of $2,000), they would sell 100 shares at $20, which would give them a 100 percent gain, and keep 100 shares to "ride free" as far as it can go.

A word about buying on margin—using credit from your broker to help finance your purchases: Some people are willing to take the chance of a margin call in order to increase their leverage. Others say that margin interest is so high that you would have to earn a great deal on your investment to make a profit.

A balanced investment portfolio would most prob- ably contain bonds as well as stocks. Bonds fall basi- cally into two categories: (1) corporate bonds, which are as credit-worthy as the issuing company, and (2) government bonds, which are as credit-worthy as the issuing municipality or the subdivision at the federal, state, regional, or local level.

One significant aspect of bonds is the rating of the bond by independent evaluating agencies. (The three most widely respected are Standard and Poor's, Moody's, and Fitch.) These agencies in effect provide a rating that is similar to what Dun and Bradstreet does for individual corporations in evaluating their credit worthiness.

In New York State, "the prudent person rule" pre- scribes that an investment be made if the issue is rated in one of four top categories: AAA, AA, A, or BAA. Anything below is not adequately secured in funding for a fiduciary (an individual who has responsibility of investing funds for someone else).

A bond is essentially a document you receive in ex- change for a loan for a certain length of time. Your reward for lending the money is the interest you re- ceive, usually twice a year. Bondholders receive their interest before stockholders get any moneys. Bonds may be for five, ten, or, in the case of long-term bonds, twenty or thirty years. However, you might want to sell your bond before maturity if market conditions are satisfactory. On the other hand, you might be forced to sell if your funds are low, and the market may not be satisfactory for your issue.

Convertible bonds, mentioned in the chart on page 98, are bonds that may be converted into common stock of the same corporation under certain specified conditions. If the market is rising, it may be very de- sirable to make the conversion.

INVESTMENT OBJECTIVES AND THEIR IMPLEMENTATION

Income	Capital Appreciation	Tax Savings	Future Security	Speculative Profit
Corporate bonds	Common stocks	Municipal bonds	Life insurance	Commodity futures
Common stocks	Mutual funds for growth	Tax-exempt trusts	Annuities	Interest rate futures
Preferred stocks	Listed options	Deferred annuities	Keogh & IRA retirement plans	Gold bullion
Convertible issues	Options funds	Tax-sheltered investments	IRA "rollovers" and distribution annuities	Common stocks
Mutual funds for income	Corporate bonds			Over-the-counter stocks
Municipal bonds	Convertible bonds and preferreds			Options
Tax-exempt trusts	New issues			High-yield bonds
Municipal bond funds	Tax shelters			Short selling
Short-term money market portfolio				
U.S. government securities & SBA loans				
Certificates of deposit				
Annuities				

A mutual fund is an investment company that continuously issues its shares and agrees to repurchase them from shareholders on demand. The moneys it receives are invested in the stock market or bond market. A big advantage of mutual funds for the small investor is that they offer diversification of investment that the small investor cannot approach. There are various types of funds. You can easily find one whose purpose meshes with yours: income, growth, or speculative, as well as those that balance all of the foregoing. However, please be reminded that the objectives of management are not always met.

The money market, mentioned in the chart under Income, is a market in which government, corporations, and banks utilize loans for short periods of time (as little as overnight and usually no longer than nine months). The loans are for large amounts of money, and interest is paid for a specified period. It can be quite a bit higher than savings bank interest when short-term interest rates are up. Most people cannot afford to enter the short-term money market by themselves. Instead, they invest in a money-market mutual fund that buys Treasury bills from government, commercial paper from corporations, and certificates of deposit from banks.

Annuities mentioned in the chart are of two types: (1) deferred for immediate tax savings and for future retirement and (2) immediate pay annuities for those who are retired and want the income now. Annuities are bought from insurance companies or brokerage firms in one lump sum or over a period of time. The sponsor guarantees to pay a certain amount each month after a specified time (usually at retirement or upon reaching a certain age). Interest is deferred until the lower-tax-bracket retirement years. An annuity guarantees you an income for life, but the amount is fixed, which may be a disadvantage during these inflationary years, which will probably continue for some time.

Options, a sophisticated investment tactic mentioned in the chart, give the right to buy or sell stock within a specified period of time. If you have an option to buy at a particular price and the stock rises, you will make a profit. If you have an option to sell a stock at a specified price within a specified period of time and if the stock price falls, you make a profit, too.

Tax incentives enacted by Congress permit investors in specific types of business to deduct certain expenses of the enterprise from their regular taxable income. Thus, an investment in tax shelters can generate tax deductions over a period of years—resulting in tax savings for the investor—while the initial investment is at work in the business. Since a tax-shelter investment should be first and foremost a promising business venture, such investments can provide attractive capital appreciation potential over a period of time in addition to tax benefits. These investments include oil and gas exploration, cattle breeding and feeding operations, real estate, and equipment leasing.

The commodities market, where one deals with raw materials—coffee, cotton, cocoa, pork bellies, etc.—on national and foreign exchanges is for the very sophisticated and very wealthy investor. Fortunes can be made in commodities; they also can be lost. Experts say you should not enter the commodities market unless you can afford to lose at least $10,000. Furthermore, you need a broker who specializes in commodity trading who can keep close tabs on such things as worldwide weather conditions, inflation, industrial trends, and political developments that affect commodities contracts. This is a very specialized area requiring a high degree of expertise and the ability to move quickly.

Interest rate futures means playing with future contracts on certain U.S. government debt securities that can be purchased as a speculation on future changes in interest rates.

A speculator, according to the chart, might buy gold bullion as a hedge against inflation. One investment firm vice-president describes hedging as "taking a position that is completely counter to everything in your investment bag. It is what will go good if everything else goes bad." If there were a national catastrophe and you were to barter, what would you barter? Gold. Diamonds. Other precious gems. Our expert declared that some people think "collectibles" such as art pieces, antique furniture and dolls, are hedgeable, but he cautioned that collectibles are only worth what someone is willing to pay, and there must be a market for that category of collectible.

Not only is investing a complicated business, but conditions are always changing in the financial community. Count on devoting a few hours each week to keeping abreast of what is going on with yours. Your stockbroker cannot do everything for you. If you asked him what your responsibilities are, he would most likely advise you as follows:

1. Read quarterly statements and annual reports of companies in which you have invested.
2. Read a general financial publication such as the *New York Times* business section and the *Wall Street Journal*.
3. Read what your stockbroker sends you in the mail.

The financial risk pyramid shows the investment picture in terms of risk. On the very bottom are your foundation investments, insurance and savings, which entail the very least amount of risk. The pyramid nar-

FINANCIAL RISK PYRAMID

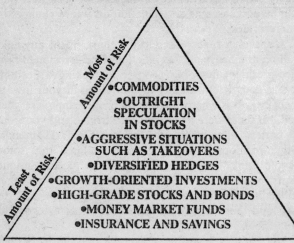

Most Amount of Risk

Least Amount of Risk

- COMMODITIES
- OUTRIGHT SPECULATION IN STOCKS
- AGGRESSIVE SITUATIONS SUCH AS TAKEOVERS
- DIVERSIFIED HEDGES
- GROWTH-ORIENTED INVESTMENTS
- HIGH-GRADE STOCKS AND BONDS
- MONEY MARKET FUNDS
- INSURANCE AND SAVINGS

rows as it goes to the top; commodities are the riskiest investment of all.

Outside of the financial risk pyramid is real estate as an investment. Since it is unique as investments go, I have devoted the entire following chapter to it.

12

Real Estate

If there is one investment that seems indigenous to women, it is real estate. Traditionally, whether because of nature or nurture, women have been more sensitive to human needs than men. And what is real estate all about but human needs? Human needs are the essence of all three forms real estate takes: residential, commercial, and vacant land. Real estate may be indigenous to women, but, if women are to profit from it, they do have to have knowledge of the basics of the business.

First, what are the main advantages of real estate as investment?

1. *Hedge against inflation.* Real estate has only appreciated over the years. While other investments have had their downs as well as their ups, real estate values have inflated commensurate with monetary inflation. Real estate is also a hedge against inflation in that you will be paying off existing mortgages in cheaper dollars as inflation increases.

2. *Good tax shelter.* In these days of high taxes, many of us need all the tax shelter we can get. Real estate gives us (a) tax deduction on mortgage and loan

interest and (b) except for vacant land, depreciation on our holdings for a tax deduction.

3. *High leverage for our investment money.* With a small amount of money in relation to what we can borrow, we can control relatively large investment holdings.

Okay, you say, sounds great, but what are the disadvantages?

1. *It is not liquid.* Even an excellent piece of real estate cannot be sold on short notice as quickly as most other investments. And a short-notice sale of real estate may mean you have to sacrifice when converting it into cash.

2. *It is not for those who are uncomfortable with debt.* As you will see, real estate investing means mortgages and loans, and that means debt. If debt makes you unduly uncomfortable, real estate is not for you.

3. *There is no central marketplace for real estate investments.* Unlike stocks and bonds, real estate does not have a New York Stock Exchange or American Stock Exchange or Pacific Coast or Chicago Exchange. Buyers and sellers have the responsibility of finding each other.

4. *There is no federal agency to regulate the sale and financing of land.*

The name of the game in real estate investment "empires" is pyramiding. Profits made on one purchase that is made by financing are applied (after current debts are paid) to the purchase of your next acquisition. The latter acquisition's profits are then applied to the purchase of still another piece of real estate, and so on. Of course, this is not usually done overnight. It takes years to build up your real estate "empire"—that, plus a bit of boldness, a bit of courage, and a modicum of astuteness!

You say that you have put away some money besides your emergency fund? It's lying in the bank collecting only 5½ percent interest and you would like to try this real estate game? Do you have enough money to get started? According to the experts, $10,000 will let you "play." What you can do, instead of being a solo investor, is combine with others to form a real estate investment group.

There are several forms of real estate investment groups, but the best form for the small investor is the simple partnership. You may have one or any number of partners. Benefits flow to you on a basis agreed to in your partnership contract (which, of course, you would have a lawyer draw up). Income is reported on a partnership tax return with deductions for interest, depreciation, and expenses. No income tax is paid with the partnership return. Instead, income along with the tax deductions flow to each partner on a prorated basis, according to each one's fractional interest in the partnership, to her individual tax return.

The one big disadvantage to a real estate partnership is that you are individually responsible for the debts of the unit. Your personal assets may have to be sacrificed if all goes badly. However, if you chose your partners carefully and use experts when it comes to matters of professional judgment, and if you invest with your head, you have little to fear.

Choose partners who are stable in their living habits and live within their incomes. If you can list among them a professional or two, such as a lawyer, a real estate broker, or a building contractor who are willing to contribute their expertise and time to the partnership on a voluntary or reduced-fee basis, you will be ahead and have more in the profit column.

That takes us to the matter of hiring professionals to advise you. The use of professionals and how to find them to help with your financial life is covered in Chapter 23, but let me state here again that something most successful men have always realized is not to stint on hiring experts. In the matter of real estate, you may very well need the advice and services of a real estate broker for buying and selling; an engineer to inspect properties before you buy; a real estate appraiser to estimate the value of the piece accurately; a real estate lawyer for buying, selling, and general advice; and an accountant to work out your cash position, handle tax problems, and estimate return on your investments.

Your partnership may decide to specialize in one type of real estate or to diversify its type of holdings. It may be that you have experience as a homeowner and would like to start out with investing in one-family homes. What would you look for in a one-family home as an investment? Most probably, some of the same things you looked for when you bought your own home. Is it in a convenient location? Is it near transportation and schools? Is the neighborhood fairly stable? Is there not an excessive amount of turnover in home ownership? Do most of the homes look well cared-for? Is the trend of the neighborhood going up rather than down? Does the home you are considering buying conform to the others in the neighborhood? Or does it stick out because it is of a very different construction or oversized or overpriced for the neighborhood and will therefore have to rent or be sold at a price that is too high in comparison to others around it, thus giving trouble renting or selling?

When it comes to investing in single-family homes, "the handyman's special" in a desirable neighborhood will bring you the most profit. A "handyman's special" is a house that is basically sound but in disrepair. Don't add luxury touches such as terraces or swimming pools, but do refurbish enough to bring it up to minimum standards of the neighborhood. If members of the partnership can do the work themselves, so much the better. Savings on painting and plastering can mean greater profits. However, remember what we said about the advisability of using experts, and don't tackle such items as complicated plumbing or wiring projects.

The month-to-month lease may be best if you are looking to rent your investment. That way you can raise rents more easily as inflation rises. Also, it is easier to evict undesirable tenants who may be destructive to your property or who default on rent. About defaulting on rent, you will want to have two or three months' rent from your tenants before they move in as security against nonpayment. And, much as we love our own dog, I feel it is wise to say "No pets" in the lease. Puppies chew woodwork and cats claw kitchen cabinets.

When considering buying two-family and up to six-family residences, look for the same things that you look for in a one-family residence: location, neighborhood, and conformity with surrounding residences.

Who is going to manage the residential units? You and your partners, we hope, because a professional real estate manager will cost at least 10 percent of your profit. Managing the units means seeing to repairs yourself or hiring a pro, collecting rents and finding new tenants to fill vacancies, and showing the units to prospective tenants. Some owners give a rental discount to a tenant in return for his managing day-to-day affairs connected with their project.

Where and how are you going to get the money to finance your purchase? You will approach a friendly banker (discussed in Chapter 23) at a savings and loan institution, which is the type of bank that specializes in financing for property. If your credit is good, if your banker believes that you have a sound building in a good neighborhood and good location, he will be delighted to lend you the money with a relatively small down payment.

On older residences you might, in order to get greater leverage with a relatively small down payment, also arrange for a second mortgage with the seller of the residential units. Be sure before you enter such an arrangement to check with your accountant that you will have enough cash flow to meet payments of the two mortgages.

Caution: Before purchasing any residential property, determine as accurately as possible how much the vacancy rate will be. Generally, a 5 percent vacancy rate is the norm. Much above that, you run into trouble meeting mortgage payments and with your cash flow.

Before buying your units, determine the vacancy rate yourself. Don't take the seller's word for it that it is only 5 percent. Demand to see rental records. Ring the doorbells of tenants and ask whether they are satisfied with their apartments. See if you get "vibes" from them about moving out.

If the vacancy rate is high, forget about the purchase and move on to another prospect. A high vacancy rate makes it difficult or even impossible to meet mortgage payments, to say nothing of coming up with a profit for yourself.

Once you get into the purchase of units larger than a sixplex, buildings with seven or more units, you are officially into apartment buildings. Generally, apartments are financed similarly to smaller holdings, as discussed earlier. As far as management is concerned, you can hire a professional real estate manager at 10 percent of your profits or, as also in the case of smaller holdings, manage the apartment building yourself. The third alternative is to give a rental discount to a resident to manage the building for you.

If you started out with investing in smaller units, you have good experience for investing in apartment buildings. You are just dealing with more units. More units, more profits—*if your vacancies are minimal.* Unless you mismanage the building terribly (and if you do, you have no right to be in real estate), you should not have a high vacancy rate. Look at it this way: If the building did have a high vacancy rate when you bought it, the bank would not have loaned you the money because it would have figured it as a bad risk.

Don't overlook old buildings when you are looking to purchase. You may be able to get a rehabilitation financing loan insured by the federal government. Ask your friendly banker at the savings and loan about that. Some states grant aid to rehabilitation by deferring property taxes for a certain number of years. Ask your friendly banker about that, too.

Commercial real estate is a different ball game, but not that forbidding if you stick to the small office or professional building. We are talking about the single-story building that does not require an elevator (elevator office buildings are in a different, higher-price category). Rent is calculated as so much per foot in office buildings. An older building would rent for much less per foot than a brand-new building. Consequently, the financing for an older building will be less than for the construction of a new one. (We strongly recommend that you steer clear of construction of your own anyway, because it is to risky.)

You most probably will rent offices out on three-year leases with options to renew at a rate that increases with the cost of living index plus tax increases. You will have to provide janitor service, but there are usually janitor service companies you can assign that task. Usually you provide utilities, but if you have a tenant with special requirements, such as a radiologist, you may ask the tenant to provide his own utilities, which would entail, say, electrical wiring zoning to meet his special needs.

Once professional and medical buildings are rented, if tenants are happy, there are few vacancies. These tenants hate to move because, of course, a change of address always means lost time for them and also may mean leaving some clients and patients behind. Generally, too, they are prompt with rent payment.

Real estate experts are reporting that the huge regional shopping malls of suburban and exurban areas are experiencing a new challenge from smaller neighborhood and community strip centers because of the energy crisis. The smaller strip shopping centers are what are attractive to the small investor. The smaller the shopping center, the simpler the financing and also the easier it is to raise rents because you are not so dependent on the large anchor tenants who can negotiate rental discounts. The small store will pay the high rent and often a percentage of its gross profits as stipulated in its lease. Usually, the percentage of profits paid goes up with the percentage of the markup. A jeweler with a high markup would pay a higher percentage to you on his gross receipts than, say, a bargain clothing store.

Vacant land is held for capital appreciation. Some say that if you hold vacant land long enough, it is bound to appreciate even if it is in the wilds of Wisconsin. Palm Springs is built in a desert, and Miami Beach was once swampland! The vacant land is held for appreciation and sold if the price and terms are agreeable to you for a capital gain that is reported on your income tax. If it is a long-term gain (if you have had the property more than one year), tax paid on the gain is 40 percent of ordinary income.

Of course, understand that while you are holding the land, hoping it appreciates, you are paying interest on the loan that helped you buy it and you are also paying property taxes, but you do not earn rental income because there are no buildings on the land. However, some people farm on the land and do make some profit on that. Some experts say that to depend on income from farming to defray the cost of loan and taxes is chancy because most farms these days are one-crop farms, thus putting you in the commodities business, which is a risky one indeed. Perhaps you should, when you think of farming your land, think in terms of multi-crop.

Before you buy a piece of vacant land, investigate zoning laws and whether or not there is a master plan for the community where it is located so that you will know whether your vacant land is destined for, say, suburban housing or light industry.

You must also ask yourself two questions: How soon will this property be in short supply? and Whom will I be able to sell this land to? After all, your aim is a capital gain, and if you are to realize that, you must be able to come up with good positive answers to those questions.

We have talked about your buying real estate but not about how to find real estate to purchase. The most obvious way is through a real estate broker. If you have one in your investment group, marvelous, because brokerage fees run from 5 to 10 percent or more, and that is based on purchase price. Whether you pay the fee or the seller does, you most certainly will be paying for it in the end. A note: Even if you find a piece of real estate yourself, if it is listed with a broker, you must pay the broker's fee.

Another way to find property is to advertise in newspapers for what you want. "Property Wanted" ads are scanned by sellers for exactly this purpose. Still a third way to find real estate property is, when you happen to spot something you like, to directly approach the owner or his lawyer, stating your intent and making a proposition. The owner may very well take you up on your offer after a certain amount of negotiating back and forth. Your own community may be undergoing zoning changes or rehabilitation in certain quarters, or perhaps a new road is built that makes a particular piece of property attractive. Make an offer to the owner.

Sometimes there is what is called a "distress sale" on property. Someone is forced to sell because he cannot meet taxes. There may even be a tax lien on the property. In the latter case, there is usually an auction for prospective buyers. Good buys can be made at these auctions, but you have to know what you are doing. Appraise the property or have it appraised before you go to the auction. Decide what your firm top price is, and *do not get carried away in bidding*. Because you must pay cash in full at these sales, you have to do your financing *before* the sale. What you might do is take out a short-term loan to cover your proposed top bid and then, if you do get the property, arrange for a long-term loan on easier terms.

A few words about options. Suppose you have seen a piece of property that has strong appeal. You want to investigate a few things about it and you want to put your feelers out for long-term financing, but you don't want to risk losing the property to someone else. In that case you may ask the seller for an option. An option is the right to buy within a specified period of time. It is secured with an agreed-upon payment that is applied to the purchase price if you exercise your option. If, through no fault of the seller, you do not, you forfeit the option money.

This chapter has given the basics of real estate investment. We advise that before you plunge in, you read all the books you can put your hands on about real estate and consider taking one of the real estate investment courses offered by continuing education departments of colleges and universities or your local school system adult education department.

Important to the investor in anything is knowing how to read a profit-and-loss statement. The next chapter tells how.

13

Learning to Read
a Profit-and-Loss Statement

Why is it important to be able to read a profit-and-loss statement? Why should you even bother to learn how to read one? There are several reasons. Like many women today, you may be investing in the corporation for which you work and want to know how that corporation operates financially. Like many women, you may be involved in the stock market and may be sent financial reports of corporations in whose stock you have invested that include a profit-and-loss statement. Volunteer and social organizations may present financial statements of account, and civic organizations are also required to file financial statements and make them available for public scrutiny, all of which will contain operating figures.

What is a profit-and-loss statement? Briefly, it is an income statement. It contains an account of the profits (or earnings) and loss (the cost of goods or services) for a fixed period of time.

For purposes of comparison, most corporations in their financial reports will show the contrast of the present year ending at a specified date and the earnings of a previous year ending at the same specified date.

Let us take as an example a fictitious company, Amalgamated Manufacturing, which has issued an in-

Amalgamated Manufacturing Corp.
Income Statement
for Period Ending Dec. 31

	Income	1980 Amount in Thousands	1981 Amount in Thousands
1.	Sales	1,107,968	918,570
2.	Sales discounts	16,893	12,612
3.	Returns and allowances	17,304	16,822
4.	Total income from sales	1,073,771	889,136
5.	Cost of sales	746,786	546,844
6.	Gross profit	326,985	342,292
	Operating expenses		
7.	Selling expenses	30,097	41,133
8.	General and administrative expenses	272,689	267,942
9.	Total operating expenses	302,786	309,075
10.	Net operating income	24,199	33,217
11.	Other income	475	445
12.	Net income	24,674	33,662
13.	Less interest on bonds	686	672
	Income before taxes	23,988	32,990
14.	Provision for federal tax	1,065	5,572
15.	NET PROFIT FOR YEAR	22,923	27,418

come statement for year ending December 31, 1981. It is contrasted with the income for the year ending December 31, 1980. The income statement is in condensed form. Such a condensed statement ordinarily provides enough information for all interested groups except management. Some company statements are expanded, or supplemental schedules may be prepared to present details of the cost of merchandise sold, selling expenses, general expenses, other income, and other expenses.

What Amalgamated is attempting to show in its 1981 year report is a comparison of amounts received from the sale of goods with the cost of manufacture and of operating the corporation to produce those sales. The 1981 figures are presented alongside 1980 figures for purposes of comparing how Amalgamated did financially in the two periods. The most important source of income for the corporation is, of course, its total income from (1) *sales*. (If the corporation is a service organization rather than a manufacturing one, net sales would be translated as operating revenue.)

(2) *Sales discounts* (discounts given to customers for prompt payment) and (3) *returns and allowances for credit* are subtracted from sales to produce the figure for (4) *total income from sales*. (If our corporation was a service organization rather than a manufacturing one, total income from sales would be translated as total operating revenue.)

(5) *Cost of sales* represents the cost of manufacturing the goods. It might include purchase of raw materials, direct labor (labor directly involved in the manufacturing of the goods), indirect labor (supervisory personnel), depreciation of machinery used in manufacturing chargeable against expense of production, payroll taxes, union assessments, and other factory expenses such as power, cost of small tools, and anything else used in manufacturing that cannot be seen in the product. Subtracting cost of sales from total income from sales gives us the gross profit or loss. In Amalgamated's case, happily, it is (6) *gross profit*.

Operating expenses, which include (7) *selling expenses* and (8) *general and administrative expenses,* are subtracted from gross profit to give (9) *total operating expenses.* Selling expenses might be advertising, automobile expenses, sales commissions, cost of credit checking and collections, shipping expenses, postage, travel, and entertainment. General and administrative expenses might be officers' salaries and expenses, office employee salaries and expenses, accounting, bank charges, legal fees, and equipment rental.

(10) *Net operating income* is what the corporation has after all operating expenses are deducted from gross profit.

A large corporation such as Amalgamated may have income from sources other than sales. That income may be dividends and interest from its investments in stocks and bonds. This item is usually called simply (11) *other income* or miscellaneous income. When it is combined with operating income, we get the corporation's (12) *net income.* Income sources are called plus factors.

Now for minus factors. What are those minus factors we must deduct from Amalgamated's plus factors? Besides the already accounted-for cost of sales and operating expenses, there is interest paid to its bondholders. (13) *Bond interest* is a fixed charge. That is, it must be paid yearly whether the corporation is making money or not. Provision must also be made for (14) *federal income tax* on this basis: 20 percent on the first $25,000: 22 percent on the next $20,000; 48 percent on the excess over that, less investment and job incentive credits if applicable.

After all income or plus factors have been accounted for and all costs and expenses or the minus factors have been arrived at, the difference overall is the net income for Amalgamated—in this case, (15) *net profit for the year*.

Financial reports sometimes include footnotes. Take special note of them. Legal requirements say that footnotes must be in type as large as the numbers in the report. Do not neglect to read footnotes. They may reveal a great deal about the financial story of the corporation. They may tell you, for instance, that the company's method of depreciation of fixed assets has been changed from straight life to accelerated, or perhaps that changes in foreign currency evaluation have resulted in a certain percentage of change in gain or loss to the company. On the darker side, a footnote may even tell you that the corporation has become insolvent.

Now that you know how to read a financial statement, you can go about analyzing it to find out whether a corporation represents a good investment for you. First you might look at its *operating margin of profit*. This is figured by dividing net operating income by total income from sales. This will give us the percentage of the margin of profit. Taking Amalgamated's figures, we calculate thusly:

$$1980 \ \frac{24,199}{1,073,771} = 2.25\% \quad 1981 \ \frac{33,217}{889,136} = 3.74\%$$

Our operating margin of profit percentage means that for each $100 of sales there remained $2.25 of net operating income in 1980 contrasted with $3.74 for 1981.

Operating cost percentage is another indication that one might use to judge the health of a corporation. The operating cost percentage is the complement of margin of profit. It is determined by comparing percentage of sales to total operating costs. Thus:

	1980	Ratio (%)	1981	Ratio (%)
Total income sales	1,073,771	100	889,136	100
Total income costs	1,049,572	97.75	855,919	96.26
Operating income	24,199	2.25	33,217	3.74

In the Amalgamated statement, the total income costs would be the sum of lines 5 and 9.

Net profit ratio is a third method of determining the health of a corporation. It is calculated by dividing the net profit by the total income from sales.

$$\frac{1980}{} \qquad \frac{1981}{}$$

$$\frac{22,923}{1,073,771} = 2.13\% \qquad \frac{27,418}{889,136} = 3.08\%$$

To really judge whether Amalgamated did well in 1981, we would want to compare all of Amalgamated's percentages for that date with those for 1980. Amalgamated's statement reflects our inflationary times. It showed a smaller net profit in 1981 than in 1980, although it increased sales because of price increases on additional units sold while its cost of operations increased disproportionately.

We would also want to compare our Amalgamated's percentages with those of corporations in the same field of manufacture or operation to see if they are on a par with or higher than those in the same field.

The wise investor will take into account factors other than those deduced from financial statements. She must consider current national economic conditions and those for her corporation's industry as well as current and proposed management policies for her particular corporation. Obtaining this information requires close reading of the financial pages of a large city daily, or it may be gleaned through subscribing to a financial research organization.

The next chapter deals with an important aspect of your financial life: insurance.

14

Insurance

If you draw a blank when it comes to the topic of insurance, you are in good company. Most people, including all those seemingly knowledgeable males you know, are just as ignorant, misinformed, and confused about it as you are. And why not, when you consider, for example, that one major company alone has forty-nine life insurance policies and prices offering the same death benefit!

The average person depends on an insurance agent to guide her through the confusion of this plethora of policies to the one that is best for her. However, because your agent is not entirely without self-interest—his commission is based on the policy he sells you—it certainly is to your advantage to be armed with knowledge of the fundamentals so that you can at least come to an intelligent decision on what coverage you need at the best price.

First, do you need life insurance at all? If you are a single woman without dependents, you probably don't need any life insurance since life insurance is mainly to replace income for someone else. And as for funeral expenses, most likely you have enough in savings to cover those. If perchance you are a single woman who has a half-millon-dollar estate and no marital deduction, you might want insurance to cover the $110,000 that will be levied in estate taxes so that your heirs, say a favorite niece or nephew or a specified charity, would not have that tax biting into their inheritance.

A single woman with dependent parents, siblings, or children should have life insurance to replace the income they are dependent on. A married woman without children might have life insurance if her husband depends on her income for them to maintain a certain standard of living. Certainly she would want life insurance if her husband is incapacitated in some way so that he is completely dependent on her.

A young homemaker with children, though she may not be part of the work force, should have life insurance, too. Her premature death could mean paying as much as $8,000 per year to a housekeeper. She would need to be insured for $40,000 to $50,000 to cover the cost of replacing her services in the house until the children are old enough to take care of themselves. This is a case not of replacing income but of replacing cost of care.

The married working woman with children may be working simply to help put food on the table or to help meet future goals for the family, such as college educations for the children. In either case, life insurance should be in the picture.

There are three basic types of life insurance: term, whole life, and endowment.

Term insurance provides temporary protection since it covers you only for a certain period of time. It can be either for a stated period of years or to a specific age. Usually term policies are written for five or ten years. There is no savings element in them. You get nothing back after the term is up. However, you may renew it regardless of the state of your health, although the amount you pay—the premium—will be higher as you get older. Term offers young people the most life insurance protection at the lowest dollar outlay. After age forty-five, term insurance premiums are much higher, but since most of your financial responsibilities toward your children are behind you, you may want to reduce the amount of term you are carrying.

"Decreasing" term is a type of term insurance you might want to consider. Under this type of policy, protection gradually decreases over time. It is often used as mortgage insurance, since at any point in time the policy's protection is approximately the same as the remaining balance of the mortgage. If you were to die, the policy would pay off the mortgage, leaving your house clear of debt.

If you do buy term insurance, do make sure that it is convertible to a different type of policy if you ever want to make a switch. It should be convertible to whole life no matter what happens to your health and should be convertible at standard rates, though the cost of the new policy would be higher, depending on the amount and the type of contract you select.

Why would you want to switch to whole life when you get older? Because whole life's premiums remain the same even though you are growing older, and also because whole life has "cash value." The cash value grows as you pay your premiums. A table in each policy shows the cash value at various times in the life of the policy that you would get if you give up or "surrender" the policy for cash.

Why would you be interested in cash value? When you reach retirement, you may feel that additional income is more important than insurance protection. You can then surrender your policy to the company and use the amount of cash value to provide a regular monthly income. On the other hand, you may still want to keep some protection but want to stop paying premiums when you reach retirement age. You have two choices: (1) Convert your policy into one that is fully paid up with a smaller face value that will cover you as long as you live, or (2) convert it into "extended term" insurance—a policy for the same amount as the previous policy but that provides insurance only for a specified length of time, after which it ends.

The cash value of your policy may be used as collateral for borrowing. You can borrow up to the amount of the accumulated cash value from your insurance policy. The interest rate is stated in your policy. Of course, the amount of the loan plus interest is subtracted from the death payment, so that if you die before repaying the loan, your heirs will receive that much less. You would only want to use the loan feature in times of emergency and repay it back as soon as possible.

You might want to consider a "combination policy" that includes term insurance and whole life in one package. As a package, the combination costs less than if term and whole life were purchased separately. Heads of households might want to consider a combination policy that combines whole life insurance with decreasing term insurance for a certain number of years. This would give your dependents income during their young years as well as a lump sum payment. After a certain number of years, say twenty, the term insurance ends and with it your premiums are reduced, but the face value still continues.

The third type of life insurance, endowment, combines savings with life insurance. An endowment policy is taken out for a certain length of time, usually for a specific purpose—say for your child's college education. Some people make the mistake of taking the endowment policy out on the child's life. Why is that a mistake? You are putting money away in the form of premiums for the child's education. The savings cost is high because it carries life insurance that guarantees that on death of the insured the face value of the policy would be paid. If the child dies, you would, of course, not need the money for his or her education. It is better to take the endowment policy out on the life of the breadwinner. Then, if the breadwinner dies before the end of the policy, the child is still guaranteed a certain amount (the face value of the policy) toward his or her education.

Instead of paying the relatively high premiums of endowments, it might be wiser to increase term insurance and also to set up a specific college savings fund in a bank at the highest interest available.

If you are young and your budget is limited, the most important thing to remember about life insurance is to buy as much term as you can rather than buy the more expensive whole. The term will cover you during those years when your children need your protection the most.

Health Insurance

Health insurance is up there with life insurance as a necessity of everyday life today. Hospital and medical costs have zoomed up at such an astronomical rate that one serious illness can wipe out the savings of even the relatively affluent.

Everyone should have basic coverage for hospitalization and for surgery. Blue Cross/Blue Shield will provide this for you, and you should by all means try to get coverage in a group, which is cheaper than individual. If your firm does not offer group coverage, possibly you can get it through your union, professional organization, or fraternal organization. Group coverage costs 15 to 40 percent less than individual coverage.

You also should have major medical insurance. This insurance coverage pays for most types of care in and out of a hospital. It picks up where basic coverage leaves off. Usually, the maximum on major medical policies is $250,000. Here again, look for group coverage, which is much less costly than individual coverage. You might also take the largest deductible that you can to keep your insurance policy cost down. After all, it is the really large bills you want paid; you can usually manage, say, to find $1,000 to pay your medical bills.

To give you an example of how much major medical might cost, one policy offers $250,000 in benefit limit with a deductible of $1,000. The cost for an individual woman at age thirty would be $404.87; at age 40, it is $488.06, and at age fifty, it is $600.48. The plan pays 80 percent reimbursement of all covered hospital and medical charges for each covered person and for each unrelated injury or sickness beyond the deductible amount (chosen by you when you sign up for the policy) up to the benefit limit (benefit limit depends on which policy you sign up for). Outpatient psychiatric treatment will be covered for no more than ninety days in a benefit period.

One hundred percent reimbursement will be made for the remainder of the benefit period when a covered person incurs out-of-pocket expenses (other than those used to satisfy the deductible) of $5,000 for covered charges reimbursable at 80 percent.

There is 50 percent reimbursement of all covered charges for each covered person and for each unrelated injury or sickness beyond the deductible amount up to the maximum benefit limit for charges in connection with:

1. Charges for room, board, medical services, and supplies in an accredited facility primarily for drug addiction, alcoholism, treatment of mental or nervous diseases or disorders, or rehabilitation.

2. Private duty nursing service by an RN or LPN in connection with nervous or mental diseases or disorders.

3. Charges for normal maternity confinement (complications of pregnancy covered at 80 percent). Pregnancy must begin while the covered person is insured.

Disability Insurance

What would you do if you became seriously ill and were unable to work, and you or you and your children were entirely dependent on your income? One out of three workers have disability insurance. Private policies vary widely in benefits and in rates. However, before you think of investing in a private policy, first check out the various sources of disability that you might have coming to you:

1. Employer's benefits: Your company most probably has some kind of sick leave. Depending on the plan, you will get full or partial salary from this source for a certain length of time.

2. State disability insurance: Several states have an insurance fund for disability. Funds are provided by a small tax on your paycheck.

3. Social Security: If you have enough credits in Social Security, you will be covered for disability after the first five months and if your dis-

ability is expected to last at least a year. Disability payments are the same as you would get at age sixty-five, and your spouse and children may get payments, too.

Private disability insurance is basically income replacement insurance in the event that you are unable to work because of an illness or accident. The cost of this type of insurance varies with age at the time of the purchase, the amount of income coverage being insured, the length of the waiting period, and the length of the benefit period.

The waiting period is the period of time that you must be disabled before the company will begin to make payments. The benefit period is the length of time for which the company is contracted to continue to make payments to you during the period of your disability.

There is also a variance in premiums based on job classification. It costs less to insure an executive than a machinist.

The following tables of annual premiums are based on providing $1,000 per month of income for female executive class risk.

Benefits Payable To Age 65

Issue Age	Waiting Period			
	30 days	90 days	180 days	1 year
25	$408	$307	$258	$235
35	588	456	403	348
45	745	573	498	439
55	878	680	581	504

Benefits Payable For 60 Months

Issue Age	Waiting Period			
	30 days	90 days	180 days	1 year
25	$290	$173	$126	$113
35	417	260	214	185
45	543	392	326	280
55	813	608	482	434

Contracts vary considerably from insurer to insurer. Some companies will insure your ability to perform the duties of your own occupation, some your ability to work in any occupation for which you are suited by means of training and education, some your ability to perform the duties of any gainful occupation. The first, of course, is most favorable for the insured.

There are many forms of partial disability benefit riders to these policies and various other benefit additions; for example, cost of living adjustments.

Disability insurance is a complicated subject. I suggest that you contact a chartered life underwriter (CLU) who can present all the facts to you on various policies so that you can decide which is the best for you.

Property Insurance

If you own your own home, you know that it is one of your largest assets. As such, it should be protected against damage. It should be insured at 80 percent of its replacement value to be covered in case of total loss. And experts point out that with inflation and real estate values rising to new heights, it is best to review your insurance coverage every few years. You might consider an inflation guard provision in your homeowner's policy; it will automatically increase your protection by a set percentage every three months.

Your furnishings, appliances, clothing, jewelry, antiques, and paintings should all be insured for at least 50 percent of their value against fire, theft, and loss. If your basic policy does not cover all of your valuables, you can add riders. Many people photograph their valuables to make it easier to negotiate replacement value in case of fire, theft, or loss. If you rent an apartment or home, consider renter's insurance to protect your property and valuables.

If you do suffer loss through casualty or theft, you may deduct the amount that is not reimbursed by insurance and after a deductible of $100 for each happening, on your individual federal tax return.

The next chapter talks about taxes and about tax exemptions and deductions and credits that particularly pertain to you as a woman.

15

Taxes

Even Elizabeth Barrett Browning, that most romantic female, knew how devastating the subject of income taxes can be. "Pay the income tax/And break your heart upon't," she said in her lengthy poem, "Aurora Leigh." Taxes can take one-fifth or more of your income. That means that for one or more days out of five, your pay goes to Uncle Sam. Why then is it that many women plead ignorance when it comes to IRS income taxes?

You may be a housewife; why do you need to know about taxes? Well, if you sign a joint return with your husband, you are responsible, too, for anything that is on that return! Did you read the small print below the line where your signature goes? It states: "Under penalty of perjury, I declare that I have examined this return, including accompanying schedules and statements, and to the best of my knowledge and belief, it is true, correct and complete."

You may have an accountant do your taxes. Even so, you cannot leave everything up to him. The best of accountants must work from records that only you can provide.

In our book *The Complete List of IRS Tax Deductions,* we stress four basic rules you should always keep in mind when it comes to taxes:

1. If it isn't a deduction, don't spend it.
2. Take advantage of all deferrals of income.
3. Keep impeccable tax records with documentation.
4. Do tax planning every day.

My number-one rule—If it isn't a deduction, don't spend it—may seem an impractical one, and so it may be, in many cases. On the other hand, there are plenty of instances in which the three necessities of life—food, clothing, shelter—have garnered tax deductions!

Food? Tax law allows you to deduct the cost of food and beverages prescribed by your doctor for medicinal purposes in addition to or as a replacement for a normal diet. Clothing? If you must wear special clothes for work, you have a deduction. Shelter? If you have a mortgage, interest and taxes on your home are deductible.

Rule number two: Take advantage of all deferrals of income. Postpone bonuses into lower-earnings years or, even better, into your retirement years, when you will have little or no active income to pay tax on. If you are self-employed, you can defer income from a fat salary or earning year into a leaner year by postponing billing into that year.

Rule number three: Keep impeccable tax records with documentation. You might have the very best and valid right to a deduction, but if you do not have verifiable records to back it up, you will not pass the rigors of a possible audit. After all, would you argue a case in a law court without documentation and expect to win?

Keep checks and other records that back up income reports and deductions for at least three years. That is the statute of limitations for an Internal Revenue Service audit and also the length of time given you to file an amended return if you find you are entitled to a refund.

It is best to keep copies of your 1040 indefinitely. IRS has six years in which to examine your return if it suspects that you have omitted an amount that runs to more than 25 percent of the income you reported on the return. It can go back as far as it wants to if it suspects you filed a fraudulent return or if you failed to file a return.

Keep records on things of permanent value—a house, jewelry, stocks and bonds, autos—for as long as you possess them because if you sell them, you may very well have to prove their worth for a deduction, or if they are lost or stolen, you may have to prove the costs.

Remember rule number four? Do tax planning every day. Read your daily newspaper and zero in on items relating to taxes. The tax laws are always changing. Congress passes new tax acts. IRS makes new regulations. The tax court decides a case; it may be favorable for you, too! You will want to base daily financial decisions on up-to-the-minute tax news. Who knows—what was not a deduction yesterday for you may be one today!

This one chapter cannot possibly review all the angles of tax law that might apply to you. Again, I recommend that you read *The Complete List of IRS Tax Deductions* for a complete guide to tax law and pull out of it what does apply to you. This chapter will cover some income tax information that pertains particularly to women.

The way you file your return will determine which rate table you read to find your tax. You probably know about filing as a single and if you are married, filing jointly or separately; but did you know that even if you are single you may be able to file as unmarried head of household, a cheaper tax rate than single?

What are the rules for filing as unmarried head of household?

1. You must have been unmarried at the end of the tax year.
2. You must file a separate return.
3. You must have paid more than half the cost to keep up your home in the tax year. By costs, IRS means such expenses as property taxes, mortgage interest, rent, utility charges, upkeep and repair of property, property insurance, and food. Clothing, medical, education, vacation, and transportation expenses and life insurance costs do not count.
4. Your spouse, if you are married, must not have lived with you at any time during the tax year.
5. For more than six months of the tax year, your home must have been the main home of your child or stepchild.

You may also be considered head of household if certain other relatives live with you and you provide more than half of their support. Those relatives, according to IRS dictum, are brother or sister (whole or half), stepbrother or stepsister, parent, grandparent or any other ancestors of parents, stepparent (but not foster parent), nephew or niece, uncle or aunt, son- or daughter-in-law, father- or mother-in-law, sister- or brother-in-law. Except in the case of parents, you must live in the same household with your dependent.

There are a number of deductions and some credits that have special interest for women. Let us first explain the difference between a deduction and a credit. A deduction is an amount taken off that reduces gross income. A credit is a dollar-for-dollar amount (credit) against your tax liability.

IRS says that the performance of services as an employee constitutes the carrying on of a trade or business. Therefore, the rule allowing deductions that are ordinary and necessary for a business also applies to deductions of expenses that are ordinary and necessary for doing your job. This means that even if you are not in business for yourself, you may be entitled to business-related deductions.

Your expenses in looking for your first job and for subsequent jobs are deductible. Résumé typing and printing, costs of travel to interviews, and employment agency fees may be subtracted from your income. On-the-job business entertainment not reimbursed by your employer, periodical subscriptions relating to your field, traveling between customers or clients, dues and fees to related business and professional organizations, and courses taken to improve your skills in your field may also be subtracted from your income.

As we mentioned before, if you must wear special clothing for your work, that is deductible. A nurse's uniform is one example. A less obvious case is that of a saleswoman for a French couturier house who is allowed to deduct the cost of the high-fashion wardrobe she wore in the shop on the grounds that ordinarily she would not have had to wear such costly clothing.

A word about business entertainment: You must document very carefully in your business diary whom you entertained, for what reason, where you entertained them, and the amount spent. Ask for a receipt from restaurants or, if you use a charge card, hold on to the charge card receipt to prove your deduction.

The requirements for home-office deductions were tightened with the tax acts of 1976 and 1978. Previously, if you brought papers home after hours and worked in one room exclusively, you could deduct, say, one-seventh of your home maintenance costs if you lived in a seven-room house or, if in an apartment, the proportion of the rent that the space represented. Now your home office must be your *principal* place of business in order for you to get a deduction at all, and it must be used exclusively for business.

Even though you work primarily for someone else, you may, like Tina R., have a second business going at home. Tina works for a converter as a textile designer. At home she set aside one room of her apartment as her studio, where she hand-paints sweat shirts and other items for sale to sportswear shops. Tina deducts the portion of the rent attributable to that room, plus furnishings for the room and all her supplies.

The basic rule for a medical deduction is that qualifying expenses are those incurred primarily for the prevention or alleviation of a physical or mental defect or illness. Not included in this definition are expenses that benefit the general health. The trip to Acapulco you took because you are prone to winter colds won't make it. Nor will your aerobic dance class designed to keep you trim. However, if you sustained whiplash from an auto accident and your doctor recommended massages, because of your doctor's recommendation the massages would be deductible. Amounts paid for medicines and drugs obtained with or without a prescription for the prevention or alleviation of a physical or mental defect or illness are deductible, too. Aspirin would make it, but toothpaste would not. Birth-control pills or devices would make it as well as the cost of an abortion. Cosmetic surgery, though your medical plan probably does not reimburse you for it, is tax deductible. If medical expenses are included in alimony, that part of the alimony used for medical purposes is deductible.

Speaking of alimony, legal fees pertaining to the obtaining and collecting of alimony are deductible. IRS reasoning: Alimony is income, and therefore any expenses relating to the gathering of income are deductible.

Volunteers may deduct expenses incurred in volunteer work. That includes any special uniforms you must purchase, transportation costs, and out-of-pocket expenses involving your volunteer work.

This brings us to other charity deductions. A written check to a charity is clear evidence for a deduction, but if you donate a dollar or so on Sundays to the church collection plate, what proof do you have of your contribution? Put your donation in an envelope with your name on it and ask your pastor for an accounting of your donations as backup proof for your deduction.

Thank the women's movement for pressuring the federal legislature to liberalize the child-care rules. The credit allows parents to take 20 percent as a tax credit of the expenses paid for a dependent under fifteen years of age if the payments were necessary to enable the taxpayer to work. One parent may be working full time and the other may be working part time or be a full-time student, or both parents may be working part time or one spouse may be incapacitated. The 20 percent is based on a maximum of $2,000 ($400) of care expenses for one child or $4,000 ($800) for two or more children. Even if you don't get an exemption for your child because your former husband is providing child support, if you have custody of the child for more than half the year and meet all other qualifications, you may claim child-care credit.

The 1978 tax act made it possible for you to hire a relative such as a grandparent, an aunt or uncle, or a niece or nephew to babysit for you. As long as they are not dependents of yours, you can employ them and be entitled to child-care credit. Furthermore, you do not have to pay Social Security for them.

Babysitting does not have to be in your home for you to qualify for child-care credit. You can take your 20 percent of nursery school tuition up to $2,000 ($400) for one child; 20 percent of the tuition up to $4,000 ($800) for two or more children. In the same way, summer camp for an older child or children could also qualify you for child-care credit.

Our next chapter goes into the overall expenses of child care and also what to look for when searching out quality child care.

16

Child Care

It would be remiss in a book about money management for women not to discuss child care, especially when confronted with the statistic that over half the women working in the United States have children under eighteen; that four out of ten families with children under six need day care for their preschoolers, toddlers, or infants. Furthermore, all the trend data available suggest that this need will increase during the next ten years.

Many of the children who need day care come from single-parent families—single through divorce, desertion, or death—in which one parent is the sole support for the child. Many two-parent families cannot subsist without the mother's extra paycheck. In some cases, though the father's paycheck can put food on the table and a roof over their heads, it cannot provide the extras that an affluent society has come to expect—vacations, college educations, money for books and entertainments. Then there are the families that have a father who can well provide all its needs and the extras, too, but the mother truly enjoys her work and, though a large piece of her take-home pay may go toward child care, both parents view it as an investment in the continuity of a satisfying career. (And we might add that such a woman has as much right to work as the others. Indeed, it might be essential to her mental health.)

Day care comes in a variety of forms. What you choose depends on what is available in your community and how much you can afford to spend from your paycheck. The most common type of day care is provided by a relative. A grandmother, sister, or sister-in-law comes into the home or takes care of the child in her own home. Younger women relatives commonly take care of the child in their own homes with their own children. The advantage is that the child has his own play group there. He can learn from older children and feel a sense of responsibility toward the younger ones. Though the housekeeping standards in a relative's home may not be up to yours, for instance, chances are your child will be treated with warmth and cheerfulness. You, of course, have had a chance to observe how your relative acts and reacts to children and would be assured that your child is in good hands.

Another option is to have a woman come in to care for your child in your own home. This is the best alternative for infants who thrive better if there is less disruption. The baby remains in its familiar environment and the same familiar person comes in every day to care for him. The problem is to find someone with adequate training in infant care who may be relied on to show up every day before you leave for work. Furthermore, good mother substitute figures don't come cheap.

A widely used solution to the day-care problem is the family day-care home. A woman will take several children into her home. She provides play materials, lunch, and snacks. There may be a family day-care program in your community that takes the responsibility for coordinating and acting as a resource for a number of individual day-care homes. If so, contact it for a referral. In other communities not having such a program, women depend on referrals from co-worker mothers and from neighbors.

The advantage of the family day-care home is that your child is in a personal, individualized natural home atmosphere rather than an often impersonal day-care center. The disadvantage is that there is no one to observe the caretaker during the day. There is no guarantee that she is not napping while the children are plunked in front of a TV set.

Finally, there is the group day-care center for infants, toddlers, and preschoolers. The industry-based day-care center is one of the most felicitous group day-care arrangements for mothers. The company may use one of the floors of its plant or have the center in a separate building. Typically, the centers open at 7 A.M. and stay open until 5 or 6 P.M. They usually serve breakfast, a hot lunch, and two snacks to the children. Often they have a state or federal government subsidy for installing kitchens and for feeding the children. A bonus with some of the industry group day-care centers is that they provide regular medical, dental and mental health care for the children. It's a financial plus for the mother and also relieves her of time-consuming appointments while she is assured that her child is getting his health needs taken care of on a regular basis.

Because the child accompanies the mother to work, she does not have to make a detour on the way to her job to drop the child off at a center. Often, mothers are permitted to have breakfast at the center with their children and also may drop in to see them during their breaks and lunch hours. Unfortunately, not too many industries have so far taken up the idea of a day-care center for the children of employees, but those who have find that it is a plus factor in attracting and keeping personnel.

Costs are lower than run-for-profit day-care centers. Employees typically pay about 10 percent of their salaries, and the difference in actual cost of the center per child is paid by the company. Often a state department of public welfare pays for a percentage of the children.

Universities, because they have a large concentration of young people with children, often offer group day care for their students, faculty, administrators, and service employees. They are able to keep costs low because the university usually supplies the building, utilities, and janitorial costs. In many cases, the university ties its center into its education department. Students may, as part of their course requirements, assist at the day-care center without pay—another saving. Then, too, supplies for the center are usually provided from the university's store of supplies. Universities are also in a position to apply for grants to start the centers and to pay for initial equipment.

The idea of day-care centers for the children of federal employees is starting to spread. According to an expert in day care, it seemed like a natural occurrence. The machinery for identifying the need and for translating that need into action was already there. The Federal Executive Board consists of the heads of all federal agencies. The Women's Opportunity Committee is part of the Federal Executive Board, and the Federal Women's Program is one of the executive arms of the Women's Opportunity Committee. When a government center was being built in Boston, the women employees turned to the Federal Women's Program coordinator there. They thought that the idea of a day-care center in the government building should be explored. A questionnaire on the matter returned an overwhelming response to the need for a day-care center.

Some federal agencies already had day care. Among them are the Office of Education and the Department

of Labor in Washington, D.C., the Department of Social Security in Baltimore, the Department of Agriculture in Beltsville, Maryland, and the National Aero-
nautics and Space Administration in Goddard, Maryland. Unfortunately, I cannot provide an idea of
costs for these day centers, but because they are gov-
ernment-subsidized, costs would be minimal.

An example of a community-sponsored nonprofit
day-care center is one we know on the North Shore of
Long Island. It was launched over three years ago by a
group of residents responding to the need of parents
who were employed or were seeking employment, and
found themselves beset by the search for adequate child
care.

The center is open Monday through Friday, ten
hours a day from 8 A.M. to 6 P.M. twelve months a
year. It is located in an elementary school that has been
excessed by the town's school system. Children are
three to ten years old. The program services preschool,
after-kindergarten, and after-school groups. There is a
sliding scale of tuition. Children come from every
economic level. In 1978, 35 percent of the families
earned under $10,000; 48 percent earned $10,000 to
$25,000; and 17 percent earned over $25,000.

In addition to the sliding scale of parent fees and
contributions, the center receives funds from a variety
of sources such as United Community Chest, the Junior
League, and the State Department of Social Services
and Agriculture, as well as two private foundations and
Welcome Wagon and United Way.

Other community groups give aid. The local play
troupe donates ticket receipts, local merchant associations donate money, and the center parents themselves
raise money through bake sales, garage sales, letter-
writing campaigns, cocktail parties, and shows for children.

Local resident volunteers on the board of directors oversee the day-to-day running of the center. Some families receive reimbursement from the State Department of Social Services, others may receive scholarships from the center itself, and some families pay as much as $55 a week.

The center serves hot lunches during the year as well as nutritionally balanced snacks such as whole wheat pretzels and carrot sticks or apple juice and peaches. There are separate rooms for separate age groups with furniture graduated to the sizes of the children. The six- to ten-year-old after-school children, who are transported to the center by bus from their schools, use an informal recreation room furnished with a couch —a contrast to the more formal classroom setting they have been in earlier in the day. Also, the former elementary school gym and playground are open to them.

Parents should take a hard look at day care for their children before making arrangements for them. Unfortunately, too many parents look first for convenience, second for price, and third for quality. The Department of Labor estimates that out of 6.6 million preschool children of working parents, only 1.6 million are enrolled in licensed day-care programs. Besides looking for some certificate of recognition from your state as to the acceptability of a child-care center, what else should you look for?

First, look for recommendations from other working parents, your pediatrician, the local department of welfare, the local Board of Education, or a nearby college. You may find centers listed in the Yellow Pages under "Day Care" or "Nursery Schools," but do check those out carefully if you do not have recommendations for them.

Telephone each center you choose to contact and find out whether the hours meet your requirements and whether the fees and location are acceptable to you. Make an appointment to see the center in the morning when the children are not napping.

This is what to look for:

1. Ask the director and the teachers what the philosophy of the center is and observe to see whether it is implemented. Are the infants held, cuddled, and talked to, or are they left to lie in their cribs? Are toddlers free to explore a safe environment without unnecessary restrictions? Are older children engaged in purposeful activities such as painting at the easel or playing house, rather than being parked in front of a TV set? Is there a place for an older child to do his homework, and is he supervised at it? Is there time for him to engage in activities that will exercise his gross motor muscles after a day at a school desk?

2. Is the size of the group right? Most states limit class size to fifteen to twenty.

3. What is the ratio of staff to children? The Department of Health, Education, and Welfare recommends a ratio of one caretaker to from five to ten children. Caretakers should have some experience and training in caring for young children.

4. What sort of food will be served your child? About thirty states require that centers serve a noon meal, although not necessarily a hot meal. However, the noon meal must supply a third of a child's daily nutritional needs. The center should also serve nutritious snacks each morning and afternoon.

5. Are emergency and safety precautions more than adequate? Can the center reach the parents by telephone during the day? Do they require the number of at least one other person who is authorized to pick up the child? Is there a check on who picks up the child so that unauthorized persons cannot take your child? Is a physical examination required of each child before en-

rolling, and is there a registered nurse on call as well as a doctor? Has the building been checked by the local fire department for safety, and are monthly fire drills held at varying times of day?

6. Does the center carry proper insurance? Home-care providers should have a homeowner's policy with a rider covering accidents. Day-care centers should have comprehensive general liability with a premises medical payment endorsement to ensure that medical expenses will be paid for accidents that occur at the center. Is there also insurance to cover field trips off the premises?

7. Does the center allow for parent contact? Are parents permitted to visit the center while it is in operation to observe their child? Are director and teachers available for conferences with parents about particular questions the parents might have about their child's development?

There are many other things you might want to look for in day care. One parent says that she listens for a "happy hum" at day-care centers—the sound of staff and children intermingling in purposeful, happy activity with each other. That might very well be the best criterion of all!

Our federal government is slowly moving toward legislation that eases the burden of working parents faced with child-care problems. The Tax Reform Act of 1976 is a case in point. It gave the child-care credit. Under the child-care credit, which is on a separate schedule but is included with the individual 1040 tax return schedule, most working families paying for the care of a child under fifteen years old are able to realize tax savings. A working parent is allowed to deduct up to 20 percent on $2,000 ($400) spent on child care for one child and up to 20 percent on $4,000 ($800) for two or more children. Married couples must file jointly, and the children must be dependents. The one case in which a parent may take the child-care credit even if the child cannot be counted for exemption as a dependent is when the parent has custody of the child for more than half the year.

For more about the child-care credit, see Chapter 15.

Maintaining your child's health and your health is important, no doubt about that. Medical costs can run high. The next chapter deals with medical costs.

17

Health Care

Ben Jonson wrote: "O health, health! The blessing of the rich! The riches of the poor! Who can buy thee at too dear a rate, since there is no enjoying this world without thee?" We agree that there is no enjoying this world without health, but we do not agree that one must pay dear rates for it, in spite of the fact that the cost of medical care has skyrocketed beyond every other item in our budgets.

Good health habits are one of your best insurance policies for low medical costs. Eat a nutritious diet. Avoid excessive eating and overweight. Exercise vigorously at least three times a week. Do not smoke. Get the proper amount of sleep for you. Go easy on alcohol. Steer clear of the pleasure drugs. Don't fill your medicine cabinet with over-the-counter drugs. Take care of your teeth and gums daily as demonstrated at your dentist's office.

Without becoming a hypochondriac, get in the habit of monitoring your own health. Weigh yourself once a week. Sudden unexplained weight loss or gain is a signal to see a doctor. Have your gynecologist teach you breast self-examination, which you should perform monthly. Find out what, if any, diseases run in your family so that you can be screened for them during physicals, and do keep yourself informed by reading articles about major issues in health care that might affect you or your family.

If a medication is prescribed for you, find out about its possible side effects. Find out, too, if certain items in your diet might affect the efficacy of the medication. (For instance, coffee can cancel out the desired effects of medication for high blood pressure.) Also, be sure to ask your doctor how long you should take a medication, and follow his rule. Many patients have relapses, for instance, because they stop taking an antibiotic when they feel better, instead of taking it for the length of time prescribed to completely knock out the infection.

There is currently controversy over whether a complete routine annual physical is necessary. Some doctors feel that early detection of a condition may occur during a physical. Other doctors argue that really nothing much can be seen during a routine physical and that you should only go to a doctor when you suspect something is wrong. Only when there is an abnormality can a doctor detect a condition that bears watching.

As a matter of fact, many doctors agree that somewhere between 70 and 80 percent of all visits patients make to doctors are unnecessary. These visits are for self-limited ailments—the patient will recover all by herself as long as she does nothing to make the condition worse. Self-limiting conditions include such ailments as colds and flu, minor bruises and cuts, sprains and strains, and backaches due to muscle strain.

If you are unsure whether your condition requires an office visit or not, talk to your doctor on the telephone about it first. That phone call may save you the cost of an office visit. Some doctors set aside a certain specific hour for phone calls; others squeeze them in between patients. Find out your doctor's schedule on phone calls, and when in doubt about going to the office, call first. Most doctors do not charge for telephone advice.

When you choose your family physician, try to pick one who is on the staff of a hospital affiliated with a medical school. It will indicate that he is above average in competence. Also, you may very well be sent to a hospital during the course of years that you are his patient and such a hospital is usually of a higher caliber, say, than a proprietary one.

Hospital costs are astronomical. As was said in Chapter 14, no one can afford to be without hospitalization insurance. It is best to have major medical as well as Blue Cross/Blue Shield.

Another type of medical insurance is gaining in popularity across the nation. That is the Health Maintenance Organization (HMO) groups. They are prepaid health plans that provide comprehensive medical care for a fixed monthly fee. The fee is higher than conventional health insurance, but its coverage is greater and usually there is no deductible.

The federal government has been responsible for much of the growth of HMOs. Since the passage of the 1973 HMO act, companies with more than twenty-five employees have been required to offer HMO membership as a health insurance option if there is a nearby HMO that meets federal standards.

HMOs are usually organized by doctors and hospitals. They might be helped in starting by a federal grant and be given federal funds until they are self-sufficient. The flat fee you pay entitles you to a broad range of services. Doctors are on salary on HMO or are paid a division of the profits. HMOs either own a hospital or have a contract with one.

To decide whether you are better off financially with

HMO than with conventional medical coverage, add up your medical bills for last year and how much your current medical insurance covered. Then look at the HMO brochure and see what it covers for its fee. Compare the two situations. You can join an HMO regardless of your medical condition if you join as a member of a group. If you join as an individual, you must take a physical examination. A chronic condition might eliminate you from coverage, or cause your fee to be higher, or exclude that condition from coverage. However, federal law requires that there be an open enrollment period every year when anyone can join, regardless of health.

HMO believes in preventive medicine, especially for conditions that might lead to hospitalization, because hospitals are terribly expensive. You should keep that in mind, too, if you are not a member of an HMO. If a doctor recommends surgery, get an objective second opinion from a doctor who has no connections with the first. If you can cut down on hospital cost by recovering from a long illness or surgery in a nursing home, which is cheaper than a hospital, do so. Even better is to recuperate at home. Surveys have shown not only that it is cheaper than recuperating in a hospital, but that patients recover more quickly at home, where they are more apt to find tender loving care.

Contact your city or county Department of Health to find out what services are available to you at little or no cost to aid your home recovery. You might find that there is ambulance service to transport you from the hospital to home and that there are visiting nurse services, rehabilitation experts, and homemakers who will fix meals for you and do light housework until you recover.

Besides providing home care, many health departments offer free or at little cost:

General health clinics
VD clinics
Animal bite treatment
Vermin complaint and information services
Psychiatric social workers
X-ray services
Hypertension control programs
Lead poisoning programs
Preschool hearing screening
Preschool vision screening
Nutrition programs
Tuberculosis control
Physically handicapped children's programs
Blood banks
Gynecology clinics
Family planning clinics

Drugs can take a big chunk out of your medical budget. Ask your doctor to prescribe the generic equivalent for a name-brand drug if the generic drug is just as good. It will be a lot cheaper. Investigate discount drugstores, but stick to one drugstore for your prescriptions. If you have to check back on what medications you have taken in the past for your or your doctor's information, your prescription record will be in one place.

Don't fill your medicine cabinet with nonprescription drugs. Many of them are ineffective. If you do buy a nonprescription drug, do not buy the large size unless you need it. Drugs go stale or deteriorate with time. Do buy the cheapest brand of aspirin—usually the store's own—because aspirin is the same quality regardless of brand name. Sometimes doctors will give you samples of a drug for your condition and have you try it for a period to see if it is effective. You save by not having to pay for a drug that might not help you.

If you live alone or have no one who can run to the drugstore for you, you are sometimes better off with a higher-cost drugstore that delivers prescriptions.

It is estimated that 95 percent of Americans suffer from tooth decay and that 50 percent have lost teeth by the time they are sixty. Combine these statistics with the fact that dental care runs high and you will see the need for prevention of tooth troubles. Avoid sweets as much as possible. Without a doubt, immoderate sugar consumption increases the incidence of tooth decay, resulting in higher dental bills. Heredity does play a large part in determining the health of your teeth. If you have a family history of poor dental health, visit your dentist regularly (at least twice a year before you are thirty and at least once a year after that) to prevent dental problems from compounding into expensive jobs.

Brush your teeth after meals with a fluoridated toothpaste; have fluoride treatments at your dentist yearly if your water supply is not fluoridated. Fluoride cuts down dental decay dramatically. Not smoking will cut down on the risk of gum disease as well as prevent the staining of teeth.

Choose a dentist by the recommendation of a friend or relative whose judgment you respect. You might also ask your local dental society for the names of three dentists in your area. Ask for appointments, and interview each one about his methods and fees. Dental clinics are often attached to the dental schools of large universities. If you cannot afford private dental care, go to one of them. Students are supervised closely by dental school professors. If you do go to a private dentist and there is extensive dental work ahead for you, you sometimes can negotiate the fee with the dentist. At least ask him to accept payments in reasonable installments.

Mental health experts estimate that one in ten people will sometime in their lives require psychiatric care for mental illness. There is a wide variation in psychiatrists' fees, mostly depending on what area of the country you live in. Fees are usually higher in metropolitan areas.

If you feel you need a psychiatrist—and this depends on the severity of your problem and the length of time you have had mental discomfort—talk to your family doctor first. Have him examine you thoroughly for any physical problems that might be causing the mental pain. If he finds no physical cause for your discomfort, ask him to recommend a psychiatrist.

The initial visit with a psychiatrist may cost more than subsequent visits and may be longer than a regular visit, which may be from forty-five minutes to an hour, depending on how your psychiatrist works. The psychiatrist will tell you his regular charge per visit. Sometimes, if the patient cannot afford the regular charge, she can negotiate a lower fee, especially if she must see the psychiatrist several times a week.

If you cannot afford private psychiatry, call your local medical society or local mental health association. They can put you in touch with mental health clinics, which often have a sliding scale of fees based on your ability to pay. Sometimes self-help groups can give you the help you need. Call your mental health association and ask for names and addresses.

One self-help organization, with 1,000 weekly groups meeting in the United States, Canada, Puerto Rico, and several European countries, is Recovery. This association of nervous patients and former mental patients is a nonprofit, self-supporting organization. A voluntary collection is taken at each meeting, and annual memberships are available. Groups are led by a member of the group who has received leadership training.

Look in your local (or nearest large city) telephone directory for further information, or write to:

> Recovery
> 116 South Michigan Avenue
> Chicago, IL 60603

Learning to cope with stress will help you to avoid mental illness as well as some of the physical disorders that can accompany it: heart attacks, high blood pressure, ulcers, colitis, asthma, gout, migraine headaches, eczema and other skin diseases, constipation, hemorrhoids, and a host of others. According to some research we did on an article dealing with stress, the type of person best able to deal with stress is one who depends on inner resources. That person is more adaptable and flexible. She provides herself with an atmosphere she is comfortable with. She lives contentedly within her income, wherever she may be. She elicits positive responses from people around her. She does not create pressures for herself that she can't deal with easily.

Most probably the earliest childhood experiences and the ongoing experiences of growing up were pleasurable ones for the person who can cope well. And we can keep this in mind when raising our own children: She had a feeling of being loved and understood, and her parents had a happy marriage and were well-adjusted people who gave her a model of identification of what it is to be healthy and happy, therefore better equipping her to deal with stress. Her parents most probably had healthful releases for coping with stressful situations.

Our research revealed several good healthful releases:

1. Good lovemaking, preferably in a non-guilt-provoking situation

2. Involvement in your work if it gives relaxation, helps you to forget your problems, and at the same time gives a feeling of self-esteem. (On the other hand, throwing yourself into work you dislike will increase feelings of stress.)

3. Loving relationships with spouse, children, other family members, and friends providing the opportunity to talk and intermingle socially

4. Healthful involvement in athletics or hobbies such as art, collecting, gardening, reading, going to the theater or movies, listening to music, or home repair

5. Vacations, providing they do not provoke guilt or create financial drain

The federal government is subsidizing your health bills in a way, through the medical deduction allowed on your individual tax return. Medical expenses are usually deductible in the year they are paid. The government has a complicated calculation for helping you to arrive at your deduction. Basically, it is this: Medical expenses are deductible to the extent they exceed 3 percent of your adjusted gross income. However, even if you have no medical bills or don't have bills that exceed 3 percent of your adjusted gross income, you can still deduct one-half of your medical insurance up to $150.

What are the requirements for an allowance on a medical expense? Basic rule: Qualifying expenses are those incurred primarily for the prevention or alleviation of a physical or mental defect or illness. Read my book *The Complete List of IRS Tax Deductions* for a full discussion of medical deductions. You will find that such things as cosmetic surgery and birth-control pills and devices are allowable medical deductions, even though they are not strictly means of preventing or alleviating physical or mental defects or illness.

Divorce has so many ramifications for your personal financial health that we have devoted the whole next chapter to that topic.

18

Divorce

Faced with the fact that 45 percent of all marriages in the United States end in divorce and that behind that statistic lie some financial consequences for women, we would be remiss if we did not include in this book a chapter on divorce from the economic standpoint.

If you are considering divorce, you should know that it is not going to leave you as well off as you were before the divorce. As a matter of fact, even the fairest settlement, because of the extra costs of maintaining two households, is most likely going to leave you in a less steady financial position. According to a recent survey of household budgets by the Bureau of Labor Statistics, a single parent and two children plus a single person spend 12 to 43 percent more to maintain their standards of living than a couple with two children.

Then there is the cost of divorce itself. The legal costs of divorce vary with the complexities of the case. Depending on the location and expertise of the attorney, fees run from $25 to $100 an hour, possibly higher. Each day in court may cost about $500. The total bill could easily reach thousands of dollars.

If yours is an "amicable" divorce and you have worked out the terms of settlement between you, you may be able to negotiate the divorce for under $100 by buying a do-it-yourself kit containing all the necessary forms and instructions for filling them out. A legal clinic will fill them out for you for $150. However, you should know that many divorce lawyers say that they get quite a bit of business from those bungled jobs with do-it-yourself divorce kits.

Most divorces (estimates say 90 percent) are uncontested. Settlement out of court saves money. As we have shown, lawyers' court fees per day run high. Not only that, it is more beneficial to agree outside of court on the terms of the divorce, because judges do have their proclivities and you will not know beforehand whether you are getting a judge with a bias toward wives or toward husbands when it comes to custody and financial settlement.

You will save money if you and your husband can agree on terms of settlement even before you see your lawyers. That eliminates haggling on your lawyers' time, which is usually quoted per hour.

If you have very young children, they most probably will go to you as the mother, although increasingly fathers are asking for custody, and, even more increasingly, custody is divided between mother and father. Older children usually decide which parent they want to live with.

The new trend in divorce settlement is toward division of property rather than the awarding of alimony. Women today are usually expected to work to support themselves and help support the children if there are any. There might be a few years of alimony for the mother of very young children, but often it is only until the youngest child reaches school age and she can go back to work. If she has no schooling or training, the husband may provide a sum for rehabilitation so that she can enter the work world.

A woman's age, the length of the marriage, and the ages of children of the marriage usually determine alimony. In the case of a working woman who has been married ten years or less, alimony is rarely awarded. On the other hand, in the case of a woman who has been married for twenty years or more and has never worked (and divorces among long-married couples are increasing at a very rapid rate), alimony usually is awarded for life or until remarriage. Many women get around that latter stipulation by living with a boyfriend without marrying legally so that they can continue to collect alimony checks. To counter that, many husbands now stipulate in divorce settlements that alimony will cease if the former wife lives with a man for a specified period of time, or simply if she lives with a man.

The size of alimony payments usually depends on the wife's expenses, which she must list in detail, and on the ability of the husband to pay and on the amount of property allocated to her. Husbands are usually required to carry life insurance policies for the length of the support period, naming the ex-wife as beneficiary.

Re alimony awards: If a woman has wealth in her own right, in a majority of states she may be liable for alimony to a husband in some cases (for instance, if he is an invalid and unable to work).

As we said before, the trend is toward property settlements rather than the awarding of alimony. Both parties will be asked to list all assets and liabilities—not only such things as house, car, savings account, stocks and bonds, but also cash-value life insurance policies and pension funds. Then comes the decision as to what percentage of property should go to each spouse. If both work and there are no children, that decision is relatively simple. It becomes sticky when the husband works and the wife does not. In that case, the length of the marriage usually determines the percentage of division going to each spouse. In the case of long-term marriages (twenty years or more), usually each spouse gets 50 percent. In other cases, the awards usually negotiated through lawyers are 40 percent for the wife in a ten- to twenty-year marriage and one-third in marriages of less than ten years.

After the percentages are figured out, it remains to decide who will get which piece of property. Lawyers often report that negotiations break down at this point. Hassles begin over such trivia as who gets the silver spoon from the 1939 World's Fair, or over more important issues such as who gets to keep the German shepherd.

Usually, a wife with children is granted the family house. However, there might be a provision in the property settlement that the house be sold after the children have grown and are on their own, and the proceeds be divided between husband and wife. Sometimes it is stipulated that the house be sold just before the children go off to college and the proceeds used to finance their education.

Often, if the property to be divided is meager, it is supplemented with alimony. On the other hand, if the property settlement is large for the wife, she may have to accept less alimony or may get none at all.

Divorcing wives sometimes find that husbands are concealing their assets to get away with a smaller property settlement. They should know that the husband can be subpoenaed to present a complete list of his assets.

In cases where the divorcing parties want everything settled at once and over with, it is becoming popular to agree to a lump-sum settlement.

In most states, both parents are responsible for the support of children until they reach their majority, unless they marry or become self-supporting before then. Child-support payments are calculated by totaling the expenses for the child at the time of the divorce and adding provisions to that for projected expenses such as day care, summer camp, college educations, and orthodontia. Then the father adds to whatever the mother can earn toward child support, though, if the wife just makes enough to maintain herself, she will not be asked for child support.

The child-support agreement might have an escalator clause such as alimony might have. Payments will rise with the cost of living or with increases in the father's earnings.

Sometimes a husband gives much more in alimony than in child support. Why? He figures that his alimony payments are deductible on his tax return. The wife can use some of the alimony money for support of the child. You should know two things about this: (1) The practice is forbidden in some states, and (2) alimony is considered income to the wife, and she must declare it as income and be taxed on it.

If payments are to be considered alimony rather than a lump-sum settlement by IRS, four requirements must be met:

1. Payments must be required under the decree of divorce or separation, or a written instrument incident to that decree.
2. Payments must be based on the marital or family relationship.
3. Payments must be paid after the decree.
4. Payments must be periodic.

The last rule—payments must be periodic—is misleading. The word "periodic" usually refers to something that occurs at regular intervals, like the phases of the moon. But IRS has its own definition of "periodic" when it comes to tax laws concerning alimony. According to IRS dictum, periodic payments are payments of a fixed amount (for example, $100 a month) for an indefinite period, or payments of an indefinite amount (for example, 10 percent of a fluctuating income) for either a fixed or an indefinite period. They need not be made at regular intervals.

I said previously that lump-sum payments are not deductible to spouse paying or taxable as income to spouse receiving. The lump-sum rule is different, however, if that single amount is to be paid over a period of more than ten years, in approximately equal amounts. Why? The rationale is that if the wife is paid over a period of more than ten years, the money is more likely to be coming from the husband's yearly income and so tax liability is shared. Then, too, the tax on the smaller annual amount won't be so difficult for the wife to bear. The spouse making payments may deduct them, and the spouse receiving payments must include them in taxable income, as she would periodic payments. In any one year, the wife may never include in her income, nor the husband deduct from his, more than 10 percent of the principal sum.

Child support payments are not tax-deductible. Neither are they considered taxable income to the parent receiving them. However, you might very well be concerned about which of you may claim the $1,000 exemption for your child. And if you have more than one child, you may be even more concerned about who gets the exemption for the children because that will amount to several thousand in exemptions.

The basic rule on child support is that the parent who has custody of the child for more than half the year gets the exemption. However, if there is an agreement or decree that the other spouse will get the exemption and if he or she pays more than $600 for each child's support, that spouse gets the exemption.

If the spouse not having custody and having no exemption privilege in an agreement or decree provides at least $1,200 for support for each child, and if the spouse having custody cannot prove that her expenses exceed that, the noncustodial spouse can claim the exemption. If the noncustodial spouse decides to take that route, he must be prepared to prove it. There very well may be a dispute between mother and father over who provided the greater amount of support. Mother and father will have to exchange itemized statements of support. In such a case you must be careful to save canceled checks and receipts to back up your claim. Attach your statement and your spouse's to your tax return in case IRS decides to dispute your claim. If your husband does not cooperate in sending you his statement, attach your statement anyway to your return. In that way, if IRS disputes your claim, you will have a defense against negligence penalties that could be levied by IRS.

The following should be included in your itemized statement:

1. Name of child being claimed as dependent; names of both parents and their addresses and Social Security numbers
2. Number of months the child lived in each parent's home or with a person other than a parent during the year
3. Amount of child's taxable income, if any
4. Total amount of support furnished to child, including amounts furnished by persons other than parents
5. Specified amounts spent by you during the year for items that constitute support (food, shelter,

clothing, medical and dental care, education, recreation, and transportation)

Supposing you remarry and your new husband contributes to the support of your child. The stepfather's contribution is treated as a contribution by the parent he is married to.

Let's consider an example: Amy and Roger are divorced. Their child, Liza, lives with Amy. Amy remarries. Liza's support totaled $3,000 per year. Her father, Roger, contributed $1,350; Amy contributed $1,000; and James, the new stepfather, $650. Roger does not get the exemption for Liza. It goes to Amy because her contribution is combined with her new husband's, and their contributions together total more than Roger's.

To continue with taxes and your divorce: Legal fees and court costs for obtaining a divorce are nondeductible personal expenses. But legal fees paid for tax advice in connection with divorce are deductible. Legal fees for obtaining alimony are also deductible for the spouse receiving it, as are any legal fees involved in attempts to collect alimony. Ask your lawyer when billing to allocate the amount of fee between the tax advice and the nontax matters, based on the time he has spent on each, fees customarily charged for such services, and the results obtained in the divorce negotiations.

Do not be too hopeful about alimony or child support. According to a recent survey of the National Commission on the Observance of International Women's Year, only 14 percent of divorced women are awarded alimony, and of this group only 46 percent collect regularly. Among the 44 percent of all divorced women who receive child support, just 47 percent collect regularly. By the tenth year after divorce, 79 percent of all ex-husbands are not complying with child-support decrees.

The federal and some state governments run parent locator services through which an errant father can be found and made to pay child support. States may hire bill-collecting services to get the money from the father and may even seize property from him or garnish his wages. Apply at your city's office of social services or welfare if you need this type of help. Those agencies do not help you to collect back alimony, though. For this you must take your husband to court and rely on the good will of a judge to back up your claim.

There is a cheerful message for divorcees from a study by Charles W. Mueller and Hallowell Pope of the University of Iowa, presented at the recent American Sociological Association convention. They found that not only do relatively few women (20 percent) lose in socioeconomic status from their first to their second marriage, but many women (about half) actually gain. Even the presence of children, they found, did not alter the figures.

In the next chapter we deal with another category of single women: widows.

19

Widowhood

Ranking at the top on any stress scale is the loss of a husband. The emotional trauma of this is enough without the widow's having to become entangled in unnecessary financial and legal difficulties. By taking a few steps, you can ease the difficulties that you will experience if your husband should die before you.

The gathering of her husband's legal and financial papers to enable his estate to be settled is a frustrating task for a new widow. This can be avoided by planning ahead. Work with your husband. Gather up all legal and financial papers. File them in appropriate places and keep a record of where they are. This record should be duplicated and copies given to trusted relatives and associates. The record should include the location of wills, trust agreements, insurance policies, ownership records, birth certificates, and titles and deeds. Names, current addresses, and telephone numbers of relatives, business associates, and professional counselors (the family attorney, accountant, stockbroker, insurance agent, etc.) should also appear on the list. Update your list periodically and send copies to those who hold original copies.

After you contact the funeral director, he will confer

with you on (1) the type of service desired and the religious officiant, if any, (2) calling hours at the funeral chapel, (3) the place of the service, and (4) the method of final disposition (earth burial, entombment, cremation). He will also review various charges and costs, including those for items not provided by him.

The task of making decisions about funeral arrangements is easier if you and your husband have already made your wishes known to each other. You might take into consideration religious and ethnic customs and family traditions as well as family finances.

Funeral directors use various methods to quote prices. Some quote a single price including their services, the use of facilities, and the casket you have selected. Some quote two prices: one for services and facilities, the other for the casket. Some quote prices for each of the various facets of the service, the facilities used, and the casket. Most times the prices of the interment, the receptacle used for earth burial, clothing, newspaper notices, and the honorarium for clergy are quoted separately.

Prices for funerals for adults—including services, facilities, and casket—range from a minimum of about $500 to several thousand dollars.

Interment receptacles for earth burial range in price from $60 and up for wooden boxes (where permitted) to $96 to $300 for sectional concrete boxes to $250 to $3,500 for burial vaults (concrete, steel, copper, fiberglass). You should know that to reduce the possibility of a grave cave-in, cemeteries often require some form of interment receptacle other than a wooden box into which the casketed body is placed when there is an earth interment. There are other costs associated with funerals: opening and closing the grave, $50 to $300; cost of grave itself, $75 to $500; cremation costs, $35 to $200; storage of ashes in a niche, $75 to $750, and bronze urns, $200 to $250. Bronze grave markers start at about $125; granite monuments begin at about $200.

If the body is to be donated to a medical institution, the body must be needed and acceptable, and transportation of body to the institution may have to be paid. It is imperative to contact a representative of the institution for details before a donation is made.

There is also the cost of transporting the body from the place of death to the funeral establishment and/or the place where final disposition will take place. The distance to be traveled will determine the transportation cost.

Generally, the total cost of a funeral will range between $550 and $3,000, with an average cost of about $2,000.

You will have to make contact with your lawyer. (If you do not have a family lawyer, ask your local bar association to recommend the best legal service for you.) Legal advice is needed for rerecording deeds to real property, disposition of stocks and bonds and savings accounts, conservation and dispersement of the insured's estate assets, disposition of business assets, and drawing up a will for you.

Make a search for important papers. Look in safety deposit boxes, briefcases, desk and bureau drawers, safes, or any other place where important documents might have been placed. Here is what to be especially on the lookout for: life insurance policies, accident and sickness insurance policies, disability insurance policies, general insurance policies, business agreements, bankbooks, notes receivable, notes payable, security certificates, real estate deeds, wills, recent copies of income tax forms and W-2 forms, other records of earnings, Social Security number, marriage certificates, birth certificates, military discharge papers, Veterans Administration claim number, automobile registration, installment payment books. Do not discard any official-looking documents. Even life insurance policies that you might have thought lapsed may have been kept in force by an automatic arrangement stated in the policy.

The death certificate is very important. Certified copies are required for many claims, as you shall see. The funeral director usually supplies you with copies. You will need a minimum of six copies.

Usually only two forms are required by life insurance companies to establish proof of a claim: a statement of claim and a death certificate or attending physician's statement.

The claimant's certificate must be completed by the person legally entitled to receive the proceeds, who must state in what capacity he or she makes claim, whether named beneficiary, assignee, executor, administrator, guardian, trustee, or owner. If the beneficiary is a minor or is incompetent, a guardian should file the form. If proceeds are to be paid to an estate, an administrator or executor completes the form. In both cases, a certificate of appointment must be furnished.

If the named beneficiary is deceased, his or her death certificate must be furnished as additional proof.

Here are sample letters to Life Insurance Company:

Dear _____:

Please send me the necessary instructions and papers to complete a claim under policy number(s) _____ on the life of (full name), who passed away on (day, month, year).

I wish to exercise my right as beneficiary to elect settlement options.

Will you please search your file for any other coverage that the deceased may have had.

> Sincerely,
>
> (widow's signature)
>
> (typed: widow's complete name and accurate address)

Dear _____:

This is to advise you that my husband, (full name), passed away on (day, month, year). His policy number(s) was _____.
Please send me whatever documents you will require to make claim to proceeds of the policy.

I wish to exercise my right as beneficiary to elect settlement options.

Would you please search your file for any other coverages that my husband may have had.

> Sincerely,
>
> (widow's signature)
>
> (typed: widow's complete name and accurate address)

Life insurance can be paid in several ways. It is best, unless there is pressing need for it, not to take a lumpsum payment, at least not immediately. Wait until your head clears so that you will not rush into any inadequately considered financial decisions.

You may ask the insurance company for a certain amount of money to pay for immediate bills such as for the funeral, but to hold the rest of the money under the interest option with the understanding that you can withdraw any amount at any time. Interest will begin immediately on the money left with the insurance company.

Settlement options vary slightly from company to company. These are the common settlement options:

1. Interest only: Principal remains with insurance company, and interest is paid periodically. Provision can be made to withdraw any amount at any time.

2. Life income or annuity: The company guarantees to pay a stipulated benefit on set dates for lifetime of widow.

3. Fixed installments: Proceeds are paid according to the needs of the beneficiary in agreed amounts over an agreed period of time. The beneficiary has her choice of amount of money and a certain definite period of time. A young widow with children may choose a larger amount for the period of time she may go back to school to retrain and before she finds a job, and then reduce the amount. A widow in her fifties may want to choose a larger amount of money for the period until she starts to collect Social Security, and then reduce the amount.

Notifying the local Social Security office of the death as promptly as possible is one of the most important things you must do. If your husband was covered under Social Security, you are entitled to a lump-sum death benefit, but *you must apply for it*. It is not given to you automatically upon his death. In most cases, the funeral director will contact the local Social Security office. You should still visit your local Social Security office at the earliest possible time after death. Delay in applying for some benefits can mean losing them! Bring the following information or documents to the Social Security office:

1. Copy of death certificate
2. The deceased's Social Security number
3. Approximate earnings of the deceased in the year of death and the employer's name. Record of the deceased's earnings in the year previous to death (the W-2 form—a statement of earnings that accompanies the U.S. income tax form—or a copy of the previous year's self-employment tax return)
4. Marriage certificate
5. Social Security numbers of the widow and her dependent children
6. Proof of widow's age and the ages of her dependent children under age twenty-three (Birth certificates are important. However, if they cannot be found, baptism certificates or grade school records may be acceptable.)

If your husband was in federal civil service, you may be entitled to some benefits. Write the Civil Service Bureau of Retirement, Insurance, and Occupational Health, Civil Service Commission, 1900 E Street, N.W., Washington, DC 20415, for details and ask what information you must provide.

The Veterans Administration offers benefits for veterans' widows and children. Most benefits differ depending on whether or not the cause of the veteran's death was connected with military service. In either case, a $250 maximum reimbursement for burial expenses is granted. Also, you are entitled to an American flag to drape over the coffin and burial in any national cemetery, other than Arlington, Virginia. This benefit includes the grave site, actual interment, and opening, closing, and marking the grave. Even when the deceased is not buried in a national cemetery, a headstone or memorial marker is provided and is shipped to the grave site without charge.

If your husband died while on active duty (or active duty for training), inactive duty for training, or within 120 days after discharge from a service-connected cause, the six months' death gratuity is awarded. This is a lump-sum gratuity payment of six times the veteran's monthly pay, but not more than $3,000 nor less than $800.

Usually the funeral director notifies the VA insurance division of the death, and an insurance claims form is sent automatically. If the funeral director has not done that, contact the nearest VA center (for eastern United States at 500 Wissahickon Avenue, Philadelphia, PA 19010; for western United States at Fort Snelling, St. Paul, MN 55111).

The deceased's complete name and government life insurance policy number should be sent to the VA. If this number is unknown, his "c" (claim) number, his military service serial number, or the branch and dates of his military service or a copy of his service discharge papers must be supplied. The VA will assist in securing the necessary documents for the Department of Defense, if necessary.

The VA will ask you to produce (1) a copy of the death certificate if the veteran died outside of the service or outside of a VA hospital, (2) a copy of the marriage certificate, and (3) copies of the birth certificates of dependent children.

If death was service-connected, the widow, unmarried children under age eighteen, and children eighteen to twenty-three if attending a VA-approved school, certain helpless children, and dependent parents may be eligible for the Dependency and Indemnity Compensation (DIC). Payments, the same for both wartime and peacetime service-connected deaths, are determined by a schedule based directly on the pay grade of the deceased. Receipt of DIC payments will not prevent an eligible widow or dependent children from receiving death benefits payable by Social Security.

A nonservice-connected death may entitle a widow and her dependent children to pension payments. This is decided by the amount of income she is currently receiving and by the number of children she has.

The widow and her children may be eligible for financial aid for education under the War Orphans' and Widows' Educational Assistance Act. The period of entitlement for children is generally between the ages of eighteen and twenty-five. For wives, it is generally for a period of eight years.

Unremarried widows of members of the armed forces who died in service or after separation as a result of service-connected disabilities may qualify for GI loans.

In addition, widows, until remarried, are entitled to 10-point preference if applying for a position under Civil Service. If the widow is a mother of a veteran who lost his life or who became permanently and totally disabled, she also is entitled to 10-point preference.

Write, call, or visit your nearest VA regional office for further information and help in applying for veterans' benefits.

Do contact organizations of which your husband was a member. Unions, service organizations, business associations, fraternal organizations, and automobile clubs often offer life insurance policies at attractive group rates, have credit unions, return the unused portion of annual dues, and establish special funds for members and their families who are faced with the death of a member.

Most probably your husband's employer and business associates will be glad to help you. Get in touch with them and ask for information regarding group life insurance coverage, pension fund contributions, accrued vacation and sick pay, terminal pay allowances, gratuity payments, service recognition awards, unpaid commissions, disability income, credit union balance, or any other benefits coming from the work place. Check particularly the deceased's hospital, surgical, and disability coverage to see whether the widow and her dependents are still eligible for benefits and, if so, for how long. These coverages may or may not cease with the death of the insured, depending upon your husband's length of employment and the particular insurance company involved.

You may want to set up a trust for the financial protection of your children and/or a living trust for your own benefit in order to obtain professional management for your cash, securities, real estate, or other assets. Visit your bank and ask to be introduced to a trust administration officer, the individual who will assist you in your financial matters. Before entering a trust agreement, find out what fees are (usually an annual fee based on size of estate or a percentage fee based on number and size of financial transactions for the estate). If you have received $50,000 or more and have no investment experience, a trust may be the wisest thing to provide financial security for you and your children and to pay whatever remains of your property to grandchildren upon the death of your children.

Under "Social Services and Welfare Agencies" in the Yellow Pages, you will find a list of agencies that are prepared to help you with problems associated with your spouse's death.

Several organizations, such as the Red Cross and the Salvation Army, will often provide emergency funds until permanent benefits can be obtained. Family service agencies offer counseling to the widow and children during their time of need. They will recommend financial aid organizations and will even, when necessary, send a representative to assist at meetings with welfare agencies, Social Security administrators, VA administrators, etc.

Gather all current bills. Contact all companies in which the deceased had accounts payable. Installment loans, service contracts, and credit card accounts are often covered by credit life insurance, which pays off the account balance, usually up to $5,000. A financed auto or a credit card debt may become fully paid with your spouse's death because it was covered by credit life insurance.

Request a release from all banks in which you and your husband had joint accounts. This is a preliminary to your withdrawing funds from those accounts.

Banks usually stop payment on all checks as soon as they learn of the death. The bank must have the account cleared by the state tax authorities.

Change fire or other insurance policies covering property to your ownership after release from joint tenancy.

Clear titles to automobiles. Contact your state Motor Vehicle Department to learn the necessary procedure, which varies from state to state.

Within a week or ten days of your husband's death you should call the probate judge's office. A clerk there will tell you what steps to take in the probate procedure.

Probate is a procedure, established by law, for the orderly distibution of estates. It is designed to ensure that all of the property of the deceased is collected and protected, that all debts and taxes are paid, and that the persons entitled to the property receive it. The probate courts have skilled and understanding personnel who are willing and able to assist widows in completing the necessary forms.

Make this information available to probate court:

1. Husband's full name and date of death
2. A copy of your marriage certificate (If there was a previous marriage of the deceased, give this information to the court also)
3. Names and addresses of the children
4. A will, if one exists
5. Your best knowledge of your husband's assets

The probate court will publish a notice in local newspapers notifying creditors that they have three months from the published date to present claims against the estate (that is, all debts incurred before death). Widows are advised *not* to pay any claims against the estate before the three months expire unless they are sure that there is more than sufficient estate to pay all claims and all expenses of administration. If a widow is in doubt about the validity of a claim, she should consult an attorney before acting. Ordinarily, the expense of the last sickness and funeral and local taxes can be paid at once because such bills take precedence over other claims.

If there are no assets solely in the name of the deceased in excess of $5,000, then upon presentment to the probate court of proof of payment of the funeral bill, the court will authorize immediate transfer of the items, including the automobile, and the probate estate is closed. This can be done thirty days after the death, because the law provides a thirty-day waiting period before the court can take such action.

Retirement plans take preparation. The next chapter tells how to prepare for retirement.

20

Preparing for Retirement

What is your retirement dream? Leisure for painting and sketching? Time enough to perfect your needlecraft skills? A chance to read those books you've been meaning to?

Retirement dreams are beautiful, but they can turn into sour reality without financial planning. If you are in your thirties or forties, it is not too early to begin a retirement plan. However, most of us have mortgages and college bills for our children to cope with during those years so that we cannot really think in terms of retirement planning until we are into our fifties.

Financial planning must take into account that your life span will most probably be a long one. A person who was sixty-five in 1960 and consulted a life expectancy table would have seen that she could expect about 14.4 more years in which to provide an income to live on. If you are sixty-five now, statistics show that you have 16 to 17 years to provide for. And with further improvement in the prevention and treatment of cardiovascular diseases and cancer, your life expectancy will probably increase even further.

You cannot tell how many years are left for you, but in order to keep your golden years from fading fast, you will have to have enough to live on comfortably for however long your life span may be. That is no easy task when you consider that inflation will be with us for some time.

Everyone has her own definition of what living comfortably means, but you can put a definite value to that concept by computing your retirement income needs as a percentage of your current income. There will be a reduction in expenses when you retire from work because you will probably be spending less on transportation, clothing, lunches, and other daily expenses. Furthermore, you will be paying less in taxes because of lower income and the additional tax breaks available to people sixty-five years old and over.

Experts usually estimate that you will need 60 to 65 percent of your preretirement income to maintain your standard of living. However, taking into account inflation's cost of living increases, you would be wise to make your estimate 75 percent of preretirement income to maintain your standard of living.

Where will the money come from for your retirement living? The bulk of your income will come from Social Security and from your pension. Social Security, on the average, replaces 44 percent of a person's former income. However, if you earn over the maximum taxed for Social Security, benefits might replace only 35 percent. If you earn less than the maximum (under $10,000, say), 58 percent or more of your income may be replaced by Social Security.

The booklet "Estimating Your Social Security Retirement Check," which may be obtained from your local Social Security office, will give you guidelines to estimate what percentage of your income would be replaced if you retired today.

A working woman has the same rights as a man under Social Security. She can draw benefits either in her own right or as the spouse of her husband, whichever way gives her more. In order to plan for your retirement, you will want to know if you qualify for Social Security benefits and to have a reasonably accurate estimate of what your benefits will be. To obtain a statement of the amount of earnings credited to your Social Security fund, ask your local Social Security Administration office for the "Request for Statement of Earnings" postcard.

If you are self-employed, you should have submitted your Social Security payments along with your income tax. You, too, may verify the present status of your Social Security account by sending for the aforementioned postcard.

Social Security will provide Medicare when you retire. It also provides disability benefits and survivor's and children's benefits. Supplemental Security Income is available for those whose total retirement income does not meet a minimum standard.

Along with Social Security, your pension will provide the bulk of your retirement income. If you are participating in a private pension plan, you should understand it thoroughly and be able to estimate as accurately as possible what your benefits will be. If you have questions about the provisions of your plan, ask your company's personnel department for an explanation.

Find out when you get vested ("locked into") in the plan. When can you feel assured of some pension benefits when you reach retirement age? The Employee Retirement Security Act of 1974 established minimum standards for vested rights that an employer's plan must provide for its participants. As a result, some plans provide for partial vesting after as few as five years of employment, others for full vesting after as few as ten years of service. This could be an important factor in deciding to change jobs or take early retirement. If you are within six months of partial or total vesting, you might think twice before you start job hunting. And if you take a maternity leave of absence when you have only a short time to go before vesting, it might be worthwhile to return to your job long enough to earn vesting. Personnel will tell you what the eligibility rules are for your company's pension plan, how long you must work for the company, and what age you must be before you are eligible to retire with full pension benefits.

Public pension plans such as those for federal government employees contain cost-of-living escalator clauses in their pension contracts, thus mitigating the effects of inflation.

If your company does not have a pension plan, you may—thanks to the Employee Retirement Income Security Act of 1974—set up your own pension plan. The act allows you to defer taxes on pension moneys until retirement, when your tax bracket will probably be much lower. The Individual Retirement Accounts (IRAs); designed for workers whose companies do not have pension plans, allow you to put 15 percent of earnings, with a maximum yearly contribution of $1,500, into the account. You can also put money for a nonworking spouse into an IRA, with a joint maximum contribution of $1,750.

Those who are self-employed or who are in a moonlighting business can set up a Mini or Maxi Keogh Plan. The Mini Keogh is for moonlighters earning less than $5,000 per year. They can invest, tax-free, 100 percent of their earnings or $750, whichever is less, in a pension fund. Maxi Keogh plans allow 15 percent of earnings to be set aside each year or up to $7,500 tax-free. In the case of all three plans, money cannot be withdrawn without tax penalties until age fifty-nine and a half.

Keogh Plan investors may put their money into plans offered by banks, savings and loan associations, insurance companies, mutual funds, or stockbrokers. IRAs can be invested in savings certificates, mutual funds, annuities, or special government tax-free bonds.

If you withdraw Keogh or IRA money before you are fifty-nine and a half, you pay a penalty tax of 10 percent of the amounts, in addition to paying the regular income tax on the amounts. The law also provides that you must distribute the amounts by age seventy and a half. At the time of distribution, the amounts you have put away in Keogh or IRA will be taxed as received. However, you will have deferred the income into your retirement years, when your income tax brackets should be much lower.

When you receive a lump-sum distribution of your company pension, you have several alternatives regarding taxes you have to pay on these moneys. For one instance, the receiver of the lump-sum distribution to defer taxes, may, if she does it within sixty days of receiving her lump-sum distribution, reinvest ("roll over") the moneys in another qualified retirement plan. That would include an individual retirement plan, annuity, or employer plan. If employer contributions are included in the lump-sum distribution, the contributions must be contributed to the new plan to retain their tax-free status.

Jane Lawrence was employed for twenty years as a salesperson for a lingerie manufacturer. Contributions had been made by her employer for the full twenty years she had worked. The contributions were based on her earnings.

Jane was offered another job with a coat manufacturer and decided to take it. Fortunately, her pension plan did not have any restrictions on her switching to the coat manufacturing industry. The trustees of the old plan informed her that there was $75,000 in her plan vested for her.

Her options at her age—forty-three—are:

1. To leave the money with the trustees of the old employer pension plan to accumulate earnings tax free, without any additional employer principal contributions
2. To instruct the trustees to buy an annuity payable in later retirement years if that option is available under trust agreement
3. To take a lump-sum distribution and pay the taxes on the reportable income
4. To roll it into an individual retirement account where someone other than the old employer— a trustee—would be responsible for the investment made, with the option of withdrawing it before retirement age and paying the tax and penalty

Supposing in Jane's negotiation with her new employer, who also has a qualified plan, she finds that she can roll these funds into her new employer's trusteed plan. What should she do?

We assume that Jane does not need the pension moneys to live on. She must evaluate and guess what is going to happen in future years. She must evaluate the performance of her old employer's fund, her new employer's fund, and the current money market that would be available to her in an Individual Retirement Account.

There are employees who may not want to roll over their lump-sum distribution. They may want or need their money now. How can they get their money without paying excessively in taxes? There are two methods they might employ.

One method of avoiding high taxes on a lump-sum distribution is to have the entire distribution taxed as ordinary income and take advantage of the special ten-year averaging provision.

Gloria G. was forty-one and a computer programmer when she was offered a position with a second computer company. She decided to take it. It offered a larger salary, which she needed because her children would soon be starting college. Also, because she needed ready money for her children's college, she decided to take a lump-sum distribution on her 100 percent vested pension with her former employer. In order to avoid excessive taxes, which would have cut into the benefit of her move, she elected the ten-year averaging method for computing her lump-sum distribution.

A second method of taking care of a lump-sum distribution if one is not rolling it over, is to separate the distribution into two parts. The portion of the distribution that relates to pre-1974 working years is treated as a long-term capital gain. The balance of the distribution is taxed as ordinary income and is eligible for the ten-year averaging method.

Sally R. works for an advertising agency as a buyer of commercial art. She has gained knowledge of sources and customers over the years. She decides to become a self-employed artists' representative. She needs the vested $15,000 in her employer's pension plan for working capital for the new venture. The trustees of the employer plan inform her that of the $15,000 being distributed to her, $6,000 was employer-contributed prior to December 31, 1974, and the balance after that date. She checks with her professional tax preparer and decides that the pre-1974 distribution will be treated as a long-term capital gain and the post-1975 distribution will be treated as ordinary income. She also elects to take the distribution on January 2 of the following year since she assumes that the first year earnings of her new business will be meager.

The tax—both federal and state (some state tax laws do not allow ten-year averaging on state tax)—should be computed both for the ordinary income ten-year averaging method and for the long-term capital gain combined with ten-year averaging so that you can see which method results in the lowest tax cost. Usually the ordinary income ten-year averaging method should not be used if you have net long-term losses, either current or carryover, sufficient to offset the pre-1974 capital gain portion of the distribution.

On the average, Social Security and your pension funds will account for 60 percent of your retirement income. Where will the other 15 percent come from? (Remember, you must count on 75 percent of your preretirement income for a comfortable retirement that takes into account inflationary trends.)

An annuity might be used to fill in that 15 percent. You make periodic payments or one lump-sum payment to a company, commonly called a life insurance firm, which invests the money and contracts to make monthly payments to you for the rest of your life, usually starting with your retirement. Some annuities have death benefits. They will pay benefits to the surviving spouse after the death of the original annuitant, and the first $5,000 paid to the surviving spouse is usually tax-free.

An annuity might be a good idea for someone who has trouble managing and investing money or does not care to bother with it. Annuities do draw interest during your working years, and that interest is tax-free until annuity payments begin. However, you could draw a higher rate of interest by investing for yourself in low-tax or tax-deferred investments.

Another source of retirement income is savings. Savings accounts are necessary for peace of mind. Experts say that you should have a cushion of at least $10,000 in ready-access savings accounts. As little as $50 banked monthly and compounded semiannually at 6 percent will help you to reach your $10,000 goal in about twelve years.

Of course, savings account interest and interest on certificates of deposit (they carry higher interest with penalties for cashing them in before they mature) are both reportable and taxed on your individual income tax form.

You may be interested in U.S. savings bonds. E bonds pay interest in a lump sum when they are cashed in. The tax bite on that interest can be great. It may be wise to convert your E bonds to H bonds. You pay taxes on H bond interest only in the year it is earned. You may spread the tax bite over several years, and if those years are your retirement years, you will most probably be in a lower tax bracket.

Another source of income for retirement is stocks and bonds. Remember that with stocks, the first $200 of dividends ($400 if you own them jointly with your spouse) may be excluded from income reported on your 1040. If you have common stock in utilities, part of your dividend—the part that represents return of capital investment for the utility—is tax-free. Municipal bonds, though they give less in returns, are tax-free.

Real estate is another source of retirement income (covered in Chapter 12). Remember that on income-producing property, you have tax benefits of depreciation on buildings.

One of the best real estate investments for retirement can be owning the home you live in. Mortgage interest and property taxes are deductible on your tax return. Also, when you are age fifty-five or older, you may sell your home and keep up to $100,000 of the gain tax-free. It is a once-in-a-lifetime exclusion of gain on sale of a home. It cannot be repeated and it must be on your principal residence. However, you may just decide that you could sell your home, move to a more modest residence in, say, the Sun Belt, and invest the $100,000 to help finance your retirement!

You may decide that you want to take on a second career during retirement for the extra income. However, you must be careful not to endanger your Social Security payment by earning more than is allowed under your payments, and also not to boost yourself into a tax bracket that will wipe away the gains you make financially from your job or business venture.

If you do decide you want to work after retirement from your full-time present job, now—before retirement—is the time to prepare yourself. Use Chapter 5, on career planning, to help you take an inventory of your skills and what is offered in the marketplace. If you feel you need to brush up on your skills, make arrangements for your training now, before retirement. You can try out your skills by moonlighting and thus also add to your retirement nest egg. If you are thinking in terms of starting a business after retirement, contact the Small Business Administration of the federal government (the phone number of your nearest branch is in the telephone directory under "United States Government"). This agency can supply you with advice and possibly financial aid.

There are extra tax breaks when you reach age sixty-five. You will get a double exemption and, if your spouse is also age sixty-five or over, a double exemption for him, too. Your Social Security income is tax-exempt, as are veterans' pensions and disability payments. Partly exempt are pension and annuity payments to which you make a contribution. In most cases, the states, too, give tax breaks for those over age sixty-five.

Social Security plays a big part in your retirement plans. It is also a complicated subject. Our next chapter deals with various aspects of it.

21

Social Security

When Social Security monthly benefits payments were first made back in 1940, the traditional family unit consisted of a wage-earner husband and a wife who stayed at home to tend the house and children. Only 14 percent of married women worked outside the home.

Three wars, inflation, a higher divorce rate, and new perceptions of our material and emotional needs have led more women into the job market. Women now make up 42 percent of the work force. And these figures are on the rise!

Unmarried men and women who work in jobs covered by Social Security are treated equally by the system. But the commission that the secretary of Health, Education, and Welfare set up to study inequities in the Social Security system found that because salaries for women are much lower than those for men, women receive lower benefits. The average monthly benefit for a woman worker today is about $230 a month, compared with $339 a month for a man.

While a woman is working, she has Social Security disability and survivor's insurance protection, as does a man. If she becomes disabled and can't work for a year or more, she will get disability checks. Her disability payments would start with the sixth full month of her disability—there is a five-month waiting period for disability benefits—and would continue as long as she is disabled. When she has been eligible for disability payments for two consecutive years, she also will have Medicare protection.

While she works, she also earns credits toward Medicare protection for herself and her family in the event that she or they need dialysis treatment or a kidney transplant for permanent kidney failure.

Her children can get benefits, too, when she is disabled. Under the Social Security law, the term "children" includes stepchildren and legally adopted children. Monthly checks are payable to unmarried children who are under eighteen (or under twenty-two if they are full-time students) and to children who become disabled before age twenty-two and remain disabled.

Husbands of disabled workers may qualify for payments when they are sixty-two or older.

Both her widower and children can get monthly survivor's checks if a working woman should die. Survivor's checks may be payable even if she has had only one and a half years of work in the three years before she died.

If there are no children, her widower must be either sixty or older, or between fifty and sixty and disabled, to get survivor's benefits on her work record.

There's also a lump-sum death payment that can help pay funeral expenses. And if she has dependent parents aged sixty-two or older, they may be eligible for payments if she dies.

The woman who takes several years off from her job in order to raise her children finds her retirement payments lowered. Because retirement payments are based on average lifetime earnings, years away from the job pull down payments. A woman who follows such a work pattern may find that the wife's benefit based on her husband's work record is higher than the benefit payable on her own work record.

A woman (or a man, for that matter) can retire as early as age sixty-two if she is willing to take reduced benefits. The benefits are permanently reduced to take account of the longer period of time she gets checks.

Before you can get retirement checks, you must have credit for a certain amount of work covered by Social Security. The exact amount depends on your age. You earn credit in quarter-year units called quarters of coverage. The quarters need not be consecutive. The following table shows in years how much credit is needed for retirement benefits.

Work Credit for Retirement Benefits

Year You Reach Age 62	Years of Credit Needed
1975	6
1976	6¼
1977	6½
1978	6¾
1979	7
1981	7½
1983	8
1987	9
1991 or later	10

The amount of the reduction in your benefits if you retire at sixty-two depends on the number of months you receive benefits before you become sixty-five. The reduction amounts to 20 percent at sixty-two, 13⅓ percent at sixty-three, and 6⅔ percent at sixty-four.

If you wait until age sixty-five to retire, you will get

full benefits. Be sure to apply two or three months before you reach sixty-five so that you will have full Medicare protection the month you reach sixty-five. If you wait until the month you are sixty-five or later, your Medicare medical insurance coverage will be delayed at least one month.

This is important because many commercial and nonprofit health insurance plans adjust their coverage when a person reaches sixty-five to take account of Medicare. You may want to consult with your insurance agent or the office where you pay health insurance premiums to discuss your health insurance needs in relation to Medicare protection. This is particularly important if you have dependents who are covered under your present policy. Be sure, however, not to cancel any health insurance you now have for your own protection until the month your Medicare coverage begins.

Once you decide when you will retire, remember to apply for your Social Security retirement checks two or three months before you plan to stop working. This way, your benefits will start when your income from work stops.

There is another factor to consider. If you work past age sixty-five, your monthly benefit will be increased by 1 percent for each year (1/12 percent for each month) that you don't get a benefit because of your work. For people who reach sixty-five in 1982 or later, the credit will be 3 percent for each year (¼ percent for each month).

How much will you get? When you apply for benefits, your Social Security office will figure your exact benefit rate. Your rate will depend on the amount of earnings reported for you. The higher your earnings over the years, the higher your benefit rate will be.

In 1980, benefits payable to retired workers who

reached sixty-five that year ranged from $133.90 to $572 a month. The range for workers who reached sixty-two in 1980 was from $97.50 to $402.80 a month.

Once you are on the Social Security benefit rolls, your checks will increase automatically to keep pace with increases in the cost of living. Each year, living costs are compared with those of the previous year. If the cost of living has increased by 3 percent or more from one year to the next, benefit rates will be increased by the same percentage the following July.

If you are married, you can get retirement payments either on your own record or on your husband's. By the same token, your husband can get retirement benefits at age sixty-two or older either on his record or on yours. But whenever a person is eligible for benefits on more than one work record, the benefit payable is equal to the larger amount. (This rule also applies to children who are eligible for benefits when their parents retire.) When you apply for retirement benefits, the people in the Social Security office can tell you whether you will get a higher payment on your own record or on your husband's record.

A wife who has earned her own Social Security credits also has certain options at retirement. For example, suppose your husband continues to work past age sixty-five and earns too much to get benefits. Or suppose he is younger than you. You can go ahead and retire on your own record. Then, when he retires, you can take wife's payments if they would be higher.

What about the woman who has been a homemaker all her life and has never worked outside the home? She and her family have Social Security protection through her husband's work, and they can get benefits when he retires, becomes disabled, or dies. A wife who works is entitled to the same benefits as one who does not work, but she may be earning too much for benefits to be payable to her.

Regardless of your age, you can get payments when your husband becomes disabled or retires if you are caring for a child under eighteen or a disabled child who is entitled to benefits.

If you don't have a child in your care, you must be sixty-two or older to get benefits when your husband becomes disabled or retires.

If you get retirement benefits before age sixty-five, the payment amount is reduced. If you wait until age sixty-five to retire, you get the full wife's benefit, which is 50 percent of the amount your husband is entitled to at sixty-five.

Both you and your husband will have Medicare hospital insurance at age sixty-five if he is entitled to monthly benefits. You can enroll for medical insurance. You will have Medicare at age sixty-five even if your husband is younger than you and still working, provided he is at least sixty-two and files an application to establish that he will be entitled to benefits when he retires. If your husband is deceased, you will have Medicare if he would have been entitled to benefits or had worked long enough under Social Security.

(While your husband is working, he earns credits toward Medicare protection for your family in the event any of you ever needs dialysis treatment or a kidney transplant for permanent kidney failure. Also, if he becomes disabled and is entitled to benefits for two years, he would have Medicare protection.)

Widows with young children can get a widow's benefit at any age because they are caring for a child who is under eighteen. If a widow is taking care of a disabled child, regardless of his age, she is also entitled to benefits. Survivor's benefits on your husband's record are also payable to unmarried children under age twenty-two who are full-time students.

Your benefits will stop when you no longer have a child under eighteen or a disabled child in your care. Usually, your benefits also will stop if you remarry before age sixty. But benefits to your children will continue as long as they remain eligible for payments—regardless of whether you remarry.

Even if you do not have dependent children when your husband dies, you can get widow's benefits if you are sixty or older.

The amount of your monthly payment will depend on your age when you start getting benefits and the amount your deceased husband would have been entitled to or was receiving when he died.

Widows' benefits range from 71½ percent of the deceased husband's benefit amount at age sixty to 100 percent at age sixty-five. If you are disabled, you can get widow's benefits as early as age fifty, but your payments will be reduced.

Important note: If you are entitled to retirement benefits on your own work record and you receive reduced widow's benefits between ages fifty and sixty-two, your own retirement benefit at sixty-five also would be reduced.

What happens if a widow remarries? Ordinarily, she would lose her Social Security rights when she remarries. Benefits to a widow who remarries at sixty or older can continue without any reduction in the amount. If her new husband gets Social Security checks, however, she can take a wife's benefit on his record if it would be larger than her widow's payment.

What is a divorced homemaker entitled to? She can get benefits when her ex-husband starts collecting retirement or disability payments if she is sixty-two or older and was married to him for at least ten years. She may also get payments if her ex-husband dies, provided she is sixty or older (fifty if she is disabled) and she was married ten years or more or has young children who are entitled to benefits on his record.

How do you go about applying for your Social Security benefits? You can apply by phone and complete your application by mail, or you can apply in person at your nearest Social Security office.

What documents do you need? First you need your Social Security card or a record of the number.

Next you need proof of your date of birth. Social Security prefers that you submit an official record of your birth or baptism recorded early in life. If this is not possible, they ask that you submit the best evidence you have available. The best is often the oldest. If you are not sure what is acceptable, call your Social Security office and ask what kinds of documents are acceptable. Other documents that might be acceptable include school, church, state, or federal census records, insurance policies, marriage certificates, passports, employment records, military service records, children's birth certificates, and union, immigration, and naturalization documents.

You should also bring in your W-2 forms for the last two years or, if you are self-employed, copies of your self-employment tax returns for the last two years, since recent reports may not yet be in the Social Security Administration records. These forms are needed so that you can get the highest possible benefit as early as possible.

If your husband is also going to apply for benefits, he will need pretty much the same documents. It also would be a good idea to have your marriage certificate with you. If either of you was married before, you will have to provide information about the duration of the previous marriage.

If you have eligible unmarried children, you should bring their birth certificates along, together with a record of their Social Security numbers, if available.

In some situations, other records will be needed, but for most cases the aforementioned are sufficient.

What if you decide you want to work after becoming eligible for Social Security? How much can you earn without losing your Social Security check? The answer to that question depends on your age.

If you are sixty-five or older in 1981, you can earn $5,500 and receive all benefits due you for the year. This annual exempt amount will increase to $6,000 for 1982, and after that, it will increase automatically to keep pace with increases in average covered wages.

If you are under sixty-five you can earn $4,080 in one year and receive all benefits due you for the year. This annual exempt amount will increase automatically in future years to keep pace with increases in annual covered wages.

If your earnings exceed the annual exempt amount, $1 in benefits will be withheld for every $2 of earnings above the exempt amount.

What exactly is Medicare, which you are entitled to with your Social Security benefits? It is a federal health insurance program that helps millions of Americans aged sixty-five and over and many severely disabled people under sixty-five to pay the high cost of health care. It is administered by the Health Care Financing Administration. Medicare has two parts: hospital insurance and medical insurance. The hospital insurance part of Medicare helps pay for inpatient hospital care and for certain follow-up care after you leave the hospital. The medical insurance part of Medicare helps pay for your doctor's services, outpatient hospital services, and many other medical items and services not covered under hospital insurance.

Practically everyone sixty-five or older is eligible for Medicare. Also eligible are disabled people under sixty-five who have been entitled to Social Security disability benefits for twenty-four consecutive months or people insured under Social Security who need dialysis treatments or a kidney transplant because of permanent kidney failure, as might eligible spouses and children.

Anyone who is sixty-five or older or who is eligible for hospital insurance can get Medicare medical insurance. If you want medical insurance protection, you pay a monthly premium for it. It is $9.60 a month at this writing.

If you are receiving Social Security benefits, you will be automatically enrolled for medical insurance—unless you say you don't want it—at the same time you become entitled to hospital insurance.

Call any Social Security office for the booklet "A Brief Explanation of Medicare," which explains just what your hospital and medical insurance will cover.

Our next chapter deals with wills, estates, and trusts—a subject that should be of interest to you if you are in your later years, though you should really be concerned with it during your earlier years, too.

22

Wills, Estates, and Trusts

As Americans we believe in the capitalist system and the right to have our property go to whomever we wish after we are gone. Isn't it surprising, then, that one-half of those who own property in the United States fail to make wills?

We all know that someday we are going to die and that someone is going to get our property. Why should we be reluctant to make a will that will ensure that our property goes to those we choose?

In some cases it is pure lethargy. We just never "get around to it."

One young couple did not make a will because they could not decide who should be the guardian of their children if they should die while the children are minors. Thus, they left it to the state to decide who should take care of their children.

A middle-aged woman did not make a will because she was afraid that if she did, it was admitting that she would die. She was going to die eventually anyway, and this way she had no control over where her assets would go. The state would decide.

A single woman who collected Early American china did not make a will because she could not bear the idea of parting with her collection. After she died, the state would decide who would get the collection.

An elderly couple did not make a will because, though they were "disappointed" with one of their daughters and did not wish to leave her anything, they still could not bear to disinherit her. What they did not realize is that in most states each child would share equally in the estate if the parents died without a will.

Many people believe that if they die without a will their property would go automatically, say, to next of kin. This is not necessarily so. If one dies intestate (without a will), state law strictly prevails. Each state has its own laws on this, but most of the states would divide property in this manner:

- If you are single and have no children and your parents are living: Property goes to your parents. Brothers and sisters may get nothing. Close friends, such as a roommate, get nothing.
- Single, no children, parents dead: To your brothers and sisters or, if you have none, to next of kin.
- Single with children: To your children but not to stepchildren or children you may have raised but not legally adopted. Court appoints guardian for minor children and funds left for children.
- Single, no children, no other kin: Property all goes to the state.
- Married with children: Spouse may get one-third or one-half of your property and all of joint or community property. Children get two-thirds or one-half of your property. Stepchildren or children not legally adopted get nothing.
- Married without children: Your property may go partly to spouse, partly to your parents if

living. All jointly held or community property goes to spouse. In some states, spouse, parents, brothers, and sisters share property in various amounts according to statute.

Many people believe that if their property is in joint ownership—their home, stocks, bonds, bank accounts —there is no need for a will. But they are wrong. If both owners die in an auto accident at the same time, for instance, their jointly-owned property could go to someone they had never intended it to go to. Then, too, estate taxes can be higher under joint ownership of property.

If you are a single woman, you certainly need a will for the deposition of your assets at your death. Married women, especially if they are housewives, often think they do not need a will because they have never held property in their own name. They feel that if the husband has a will, that is sufficient. However, if the wife dies shortly after the husband and has no will, the state instead of the wife decides who gets the property she had inherited from her husband—property that she had most probably helped him to acquire through her services to him. Furthermore, many married women have jewelry, furs, and heirlooms. These should be distributed through a will according to the owner's wishes. Bitter resentments can arise among relatives over the parceling out of these things if there is no stipulation as to whom each item goes.

What exactly is a will? Essentially it is a declaration of a person in the manner prescribed by law whereby she prescribes the disposition of her property after death.

The person who makes a will is called the testator if a man or a testatrix if a woman. A gift of personal property by will is called a bequest or a legacy, and the person to whom it is given is known as the legatee. A gift of interests in land is called a devise, and the recipient of such a gift is known as the devisee.

It sometimes happens that the testator or testatrix wishes to change his or her will in some manner, but does not want to make an entirely new will. This is done by means of an addition known as a codicil. A codicil is a declaration in legal form subsequent to the will and constitutes a part of the will. It may add to, qualify, or revoke any or all of the provisions contained in the original instrument.

Some people think they can pen their own wills. You can, of course, but whether you know enough about the laws of your state that you can make it legally binding is doubtful. Why play with the law? For $75 to $150, unless yours is a very complicated one, you can have a lawyer draw up a legally valid will. You need not have a lawyer who specializes in wills. Every general lawyer knows how to draw up a will and how to have it witnessed so that it is accurate and valid in your state.

There are certain points you should keep in mind about wills, though details will vary from state to state, and we do recommend that you have legal counsel when it comes to your will. One point to remember is to update your will to take into account certain changes in your life. If you marry or divorce or a new baby is born into the family and you do not change your will to take the event into account, your will may become invalidated. If you move to another state, the will that was legal in your former state might have to be changed to conform to your new state's laws as to spouse's rights, witnesses, and other stipulations in statute. You might have to redo your will because of the death of a beneficiary, executor, or guardian; or you might have come into a great deal of property since your last will and have to redo it to designate who gets your latest acquisitions.

When you make your will, do not choose witnesses or executors who are a great deal older than yourself. They are liable to die before you do, causing complications and delays and extra costs when the will is probated.

Speaking of witnesses, do not choose a beneficiary as a witness for your will. That could void his legacy in many states. Do not hesitate to choose strangers to witness your will because you are afraid they will be privy to your business. The witnesses do not read the will. They simply attest to the fact that you signed the will in their presence by signing the will after you.

If you are the parent of young children, do not forget to name a guardian in your will for their protection. You may designate one person as guardian for their funds and another as the guardian who will be in charge of their physical care, if you like. If you do not name a guardian, the court is left to make the choice for you.

Instead of designating specific amounts to be left to your beneficiaries, designate percentages of your estate. Thus, if your estate increases, your beneficiaries will not be limited to specific dollar amounts.

Some people have changes of mind and heart after a will is drawn. They may make the mistake of erasing parts of the will or writing in other words. This invalidates the will. If you do change your thoughts about your will, instead of changing the original, have a lawyer redraw the will or add codicils.

Do not make insurance policies payable to your estate. If you do that, they are subject to probate and are taxable in your estate. Instead, name a beneficiary to whom the proceeds of the policy will go directly.

If you are married, your will should contain order of

death in case you and your spouse die at the same time in a common disaster. Without it, something like this could happen: John and Mary Smith both died instantly in an auto accident. They did not have a common disaster clause in their wills. The court established that Mary died first. Thus, John, who the court determined died a few minutes after, inherited all of the estate. Because they had no children, the entire estate went to John's brother, his closest of kin. Mary had loathed John's brother, a ne'er-do-well. On the other hand, Mary's sister, who had always been helpful and loving to the couple, got nothing. If John and Mary had had a common disaster clause, it would have stated who would have gotten the estate in the case of a common disaster.

After your will is written, leave a copy with your lawyer, who will keep it safe for you. It is a poor idea to put it in your safety deposit box, which may be sealed after your death, thus causing unnecessary delays in its execution. Your executor may have to go to court for permission to open the box.

Estate tax law is very complex. We will attempt to explain it, but only in general terms. You should certainly consult a lawyer for details of your particular estate problems.

What is called the "gross estate" includes (1) decedent's interest at death in all real and personal property (including foreign real property); (2) dower or courtesy interests of surviving spouse (the life estate to which every married woman or man is entitled on death of spouse—usually refers to real estate); (3) all gifts made within three years of death, except gifts (other than a life insurance policy) for which no gift tax return was required; (4) gift tax paid by decedent or the estate on any gifts made by the decedent or spouse during the three-year period prior to death; (5) transfers with retained life interest; (6) revocable transfers; (7) transfers taking effect at death if decedent retained a reversionary interest valued immediately before his death at over 5 percent of value of the property; (8) joint interests, except to the extent that the survivor can show contribution that was not received from decedent; (9) property subject to general power of appointment; (10) life insurance proceeds on decedent's life, payable to the executor or to other beneficiaries if decedent possessed incidents of ownership at death, including certain reversionary interests; and (11) survivor's interest in joint survivor's annuity in proportion that decedent contributed to cost.

In general, the taxable estate is the gross estate minus (1) funeral and administration expenses; (2) claims against the estate; (3) unpaid mortgages on property in the gross estate; (4) transfers for public, charitable, or religious uses; (5) uncompensated casualty losses; (6) the marital deduction; and (7) orphans' exclusion.

The marital deduction is $250,000 or 50 percent of the adjusted gross estate, whichever is greater.

Orphans' exclusion is a limited deduction that is allowed for property, included in the gross estate, which passes or has passed to a minor child of the decedent. The deduction applies only if the decedent does not have a surviving spouse and the child has no known surviving parent. Maximum deduction per child is $5,000 multiplied by the excess of, or difference between twenty-one over the child's age at decedent's death.

A return must be filed and tax paid within nine months after date of death if the gross estate exceeds $175,000.

You may give $3,000 per year to as many different individuals as you wish. If you file a joint return with your spouse, the amount of giving allowed without tax would double—$6,000 per year per individual. Anything above that and you must pay a gift tax, and the moneys given are applied to your gross estate with credit given for the tax paid on them.

Trusts are often set up for surviving spouses and for children, especially if they are minors. A trust is an arrangement made for the protection of property by which an authorized person or organization holds the property for the benefit of another person or organization. The property may be invested and managed by the trustee for the beneficiary. Often only the income from the trust goes to the beneficiary, and the principal is kept intact but with the provision that it may be invaded in case of certain emergencies. You can set up a trust for someone else during your lifetime. Often they are set up for the education of a minor child. There is a tax advantage in that the moneys in the trust are usually taxed at a lower rate than if it were with your yearly income on your individual income tax return.

As mentioned previously, wills, estates, and trusts are complicated business, and if you get involved in them, you should use a lawyer or tax adviser. The next chapter tells how to choose these and other members of your money management support team.

23

Your Money-Management
Support Team

Men have known for years that you have to spend money to make money. They have also known that when it comes to money management, you cannot be expert in everything. Successful male executives have always had the best in money-management support teams behind them. They do not hesitate to tell you that they owe much of their success to a clever lawyer, a skilled accountant, a shrewd stockbroker, an astute banker.

Women rarely have had such support teams behind them. Today, with the increase in professional women and with women executives and businesswomen earning larger incomes, women are just beginning to learn the importance of having a money-management support team.

To many women, a mystique surrounds those professionals. They have been a bit overawed by others who talk about consulting with their lawyers, or their accountants or their stockbrokers. Those pros have always seemed unapproachable to them. These women wonder if they will ever be important enough to be consulting with a lawyer or accountant or stockbroker. Chances are, though they don't realize it, they are important enough *now* to be consulting with such professionals and should have names, phone numbers, and addresses of such professionals listed in the back of their business diaries. Most probably these women have been intimidated by lofty titles and "buzz" words of the professions.

Do you need a money-management support team? Most probably, yes. And if you don't have need for one this instant, you would be doing yourself a great favor if you would investigate and select the pros so that if you need them in an emergency, you know exactly whom to contact. You would be secure in the knowledge that you did the selecting when you could evaluate their credentials in an unhurried manner.

Here is a list of pros you should have on your team:

Lawyer
Accountant
Stockbroker or investment adviser
Insurance person
Banker
Specialists for your particular field

I have touched on the importance of some of them and the part they play in your financial life in other chapters. Now let us discuss how to go about finding the best of them and those you will be comfortable working with.

Choosing a Lawyer

Everyone should have a general or family lawyer. Here are some of the tasks a family lawyer should be able to help with: home buying, wills and trusts, marital problems, representing you in and out of court if you should be arrested or sued or if you should decide to sue someone else, and contracts of various kinds.

You should get the names of at least three lawyers to consider using as your general lawyer. Good sources for recommendation of lawyers of good reputation are the legal counsel of the company you work for; referrals by friends, relatives, and co-workers; and referrals by your local bar association.

The next step: Research the backgrounds of the lawyers in the *Martindale-Hubbard Law Directory*. This seven-volume directory, which is found in the reference department of most libraries, contains a listing of all lawyers in the United States arranged in alphabetical order according to state and city or town. It lists addresses, phone numbers, and legal specialties and backgrounds of members of legal firms and, in some cases, rates lawyers according to their legal ability. The ratings—very high, high, and fair—are based on confidential recommendations from lawyers and judges in the city or area where the lawyer practices and at times from such sources elsewhere.

Boil your list down to three names. Call each for an appointment, asking for a brief interview so that you can consider using him or her as your general or family lawyer. Ask if there is a fee for this; there should be none, since you will only take about ten minutes of their time.

Do not be put off if the offices of the lawyer seem too luxurious for "little you." Many law firms are not above taking small cases. On the other hand, if you are told that the firm cannot handle you because your needs are too small, do not be put off. They may be able to recommend another firm that can handle you.

Bring to the interview a list of items you feel you need a lawyer for now or in the near future—such as making up your will. Ask what typical fees are for these items. There may be a flat fee, say, for a will, or the lawyer may charge by the hour.

By all means, if you are married, bring your husband along to the interview. Both of you should be comfortable with your general or family lawyer.

Thank each lawyer for the interview. After you have interviewed the three on your list, choose one who you feel will best represent your interests and with whom both you and your husband feel compatible.

Choosing an Accountant

If you are in business or in a profession, you certainly need an accountant to keep track of your financial affairs. Even if you work for someone else, you need an accountant to help file your income tax form and to supply you with opinions on tax matters throughout the year.

As a small-business woman or a professional with your own practice, you would want an accountant who could handle your small bookkeeping jobs and be available for consultation and planning and tax work. In the case of an individual who is not self-employed, you could use a tax service such as H. & R. Block for your tax return, but if it is at all complicated and if you require an accountant's tax advice all year round, you certainly should have an accountant.

How do you find an accountant? In some of the same ways you found your lawyer: If you are employed by a company, consider using their accountant; ask your lawyer to refer you to someone; ask family, friends, or co-workers whom they use; or call your state society of Certified Public Accountants and ask for names of accountants in your locale.

Call at least three accountants from your list for an interview session. There should be no charge for your interview. Ask them specifically what they can do for you, and ask whether they charge a flat fee or charge separately for each particular service they provide. If you are self-employed and the accountant will be doing your business or professional practice work, does he charge extra to do your personal income tax form? Does he charge for phone consultations?

Here again, you should bring your husband with you when you interview an accountant because his personality must be compatible for both of you.

Choosing a Stockbroker or Investment Adviser

When it comes to choosing a stockbroker or investment adviser, do not hesitate to go to the big national brokerage houses even though your investment capital is not a large amount. You may be made to feel more welcome at the larger houses, where economies of scale permit firms to profit from accounts that don't produce great revenue. Some major houses offer special services for small investors, such as cut-rate commissions. Discount brokerage houses' commissions are often less than 1 percent, unlike those of the regular houses, which are usually 2½ percent. However, the discount houses are only for those who do not need investment advice or who expect to get it elsewhere. These houses simply execute your orders. They offer no frills. You should know that many discount houses have a minimum commission of $20 to $30 per transaction, so that if you are trading under $1,000, you'll probably pay the same fees at a discount broker as you do at a regular broker.

Picking your brokerage house is no problem. Any large national firm will do well for you. The problem is in picking the account executive who will best meet your needs. How do you get the names of those? You can ask friends who are successful investors; ask your accountant, who knows account executives who have done well by his clients; and ask your lawyer, who may be privy to his clients' portfolios.

It is best to pick a broker with a bit of experience in the market during its bad days as well as its good days. He is less likely to learn his lessons with your money, as would a newcomer to the field.

You may interview brokers just as you interviewed lawyers and accountants. Let them know what your goals are and see what they suggest for you. Be suspicious of any broker who guarantees you a "killing." An honest broker will make no promises outside of helping you to make a long-range modest profit on your capital, which of course should be higher than bank interest. You may ask your broker for references from other clients. Check with a few of them. Ask about whether your broker has a tendency to encourage too much buying and selling, which may produce commissions for him but little profit for his clients.

After you have chosen your broker, check your account every six months. Compare your portfolio's performance with Standard & Poor's fifty-five-stock index. Your portfolio returns minus commissions should consistently be on a par with or above the Standard & Poor's index. If it falls far below, consider changing to a broker who will better help you to meet your investment goals.

Choosing an Insurance Agent

There is a famous saying among insurance people: "Almost no one buys insurance; nearly everyone is *sold* insurance." This makes it very difficult to tell whether the insurance sold to you is the coverage that you truly need or is the route to the biggest sales commission for your insurance person. A good insurance agent is one who offers you coverage that best fulfills your financial needs.

How do you find such an agent? Ask your accountant and your lawyer for referrals or ask friends and relatives to suggest someone they have felt comfortable with and who has serviced them well.

Screen the agents for experience. An experienced agent knows that he must rely on present clientele and referrals for a good deal of his business. Therefore, he aims to satisfy his policyholder's needs. You will want an agent who is easily accessible and will give you honest service. It is important that you be able to communicate with your agent; be able to "level" with him about your financial position and to have him "level" with you about how he can best help you. You will also want to deal with an agent who recommends insurance companies with Best's ratings of B+ or better. (*Best's Review* grades insurance companies from A++ downward. B+ is usually the lowest acceptable grade among insurance companies.)

We recommend that you seek an agent who has earned his CLU (Chartered Life Underwriter) designation. This means that he has had three years' experience as a licensed agent and has studied for an average of five years before passing the CLU tests.

Choosing a Banker

Last on our list of people on your money-management support team is your banker, but he is by no means the least. Many times in your financial life you will be called on to give your banker as a reference: when going into a new business, when opening a stock account, when applying for a credit card, when renting an apartment, just to name a few instances. Choose your banker from a large bank, and do choose someone who is the manager of a large branch, preferably the main branch. In most instances, the manager of a branch is also a vice-president. Call his secretary and ask for an appointment. Limit it to about ten minutes, so that you do not take too much of his time. Introduce yourself and tell him of your present financial circumstances and of your financial goals. Ask him if he has any advice for you as to how you can best achieve those goals.

If you are comfortable talking to him, and if his advice seems sound, open an account in his bank. If you feel he is not sufficiently interested in you, don't be discouraged; simply thank him as politely as you can and go on to introduce yourself to another vice-president of another bank. It is often a good idea to deal with a banker with whom your employer deals. Because he values your company's business, he will be anxious to please you, one of the employees who might put in a good word for his bank.

Other Professionals

Besides the five members of your money-management support team, you may need one or more others who are specialists for your business or profession or for your particular investments. Such specialists might be a real estate broker, a patent attorney, a copyright attorney, a pension specialist, and perhaps a tax lawyer. Other members of your money-management team can suggest specialists for you, or you can call your business or professional association for referrals.

24

Where and How
to Complain

Women today have learned to assert themselves in the field of consumerism. No longer should you meekly accept defective products, shoddy repairs or workmanship, or incompetent service. However, it does happen sometimes that you are stuck with one of these problems. Trying to rectify the trouble can be a hassle. According to a Ralph Nader study, consumers voice only one-third of their complaints. Don't let your complaint go by with just a grumble. Look at it this way: You have spent your hard-earned money for a product or service, and you have a right to expect what you paid for.

Protect yourself by anticipating problems. Keep sales receipts, repair orders, warranties, and canceled checks. File them in one place. They are your proof that you have purchased the item from a certain store, that repairs were promised, that a warranty was made, that you paid in full or part for a product or service. If you do not have these proofs, it is difficult if not nearly impossible to make a complaint.

The first step in complaining is to identify the problem and what you believe would be a fair settlement of your complaint. Do you feel that you would be justified in getting your money back? Would repair of the item be fair? To your way of thinking, would replacement of the article make things right? Would a financial settlement for uncompleted work be sufficient, or do you want the serviceman to complete the work he started?

After you have identified the problem and decided what would be a fair settlement, go back to the person who sold you the item or performed the service and *calmly* state the problem and what action you would like taken. Have the defective product with you or, if it is a large item such as a washing machine, have its identification number written down. Have your sales slip with you. If this first person is not helpful or does not have the authority to deal with your complaint, ask to see the supervisor or manager. Repeat the complaint —again, in a calm manner. Most problems are resolved at this level; chances are that yours will be, too. After all, most stores and servicemen rely on the good will of their customers for their reputations, and most likely they will be reasonable. However, if your demands are not met, if you are not satisfied with the response, don't give up. If the company operates nationally or the product is a national brand, write a letter to the president or the consumer relations bureau of the company. Enclose copies of all documents relating to your complaint. *Do not send originals.*

1. State your purchase
2. Name the product and serial or model number or service
3. Include the date, location, and other details of purchase
4. State the problem
5. Give the history of the problem
6. Ask for satisfaction
7. Enclose copies of all documents

8. Ask for action within a reasonable time
9. Include your address and your work and home phone numbers.

Your letter should look like this:

> Your Address
> Your City, State, Zip Code
> Date

Appropriate Person
Company Name
Street Address
City, State, Zip Code

Dear (name of company president or
    consumer relations officer):

Last week I purchased (or had repaired) a (name of product with serial or model number or service performed). I made this purchase at (location, date, and other important details of the transaction).

Unfortunately, your product (or service) has not performed satisfactorily (or the service was inadequate) because _____
_____.

Therefore, to solve the problem, I would appreciate (state the specific action you want). Enclosed are copies of my records (receipts, warranties, guarantees, canceled checks, contracts, model and serial numbers, and any other documents).

I am looking forward to your reply and resolution of my problem and will wait three weeks before seeking third-party assistance. Contact me at the above address or by phone at (home and office numbers).

> Sincerely,
>
>
> (your name)

Wait a reasonable length of time, as stated in your letter, for action on your complaint. If nothing happens or if action is not satisfactory to you, bring in a third party to help you.

If your complaint is against a local company, you might want to contact your local Better Business Bureau or your Chamber of Commerce. They cannot act as a lawyer for your complaint, but they try to negotiate some kind of settlement between you and the company through arbitration.

Another source of third-party help is your state, county, or city consumer protection agency. Those agencies will send a complaint form for you to fill out in detail and send back to them along with copies of contracts, bills of sale, guarantees, canceled checks, etc., to help process your complaint. Those agencies mediate complaints between customers and companies.

Federal regulatory agencies can be third-party help in that they can give leverage to your complaints, though they don't usually mediate directly between parties. An agency representative might tell you that your rights have been violated and advise you what you can do in your own behalf. Often, if the offending company has been put on notice that you have contacted a federal regulatory agency, it will shape up to your demands.

To find the federal agency pertinent to your complaint, go to your library reference department and ask for the *Directory of Consumer Protection and Environmental Agencies* published by Academic Media, Division of D.A.T.A. It has a subject index that will lead you to the federal agency you want.

Often a complaint to the trade or business association related to your deficient purchase or service will help you resolve your problem. Ask in your library reference department for the *Encyclopedia of Associa-*

tions published by Gale Research Co. or the *National Trade and Professional Associations of the United States and Canada,* published by Columbia Books, Inc. The latter has a key word index.

Most reference departments of libraries have a great many paperbacks and pamphlets concerning consumerism that list agencies that can help you deal with your problem.

If your letters, phone calls, and third-party agencies have not helped you resolve your problem, you might sue. Suing can be a hassle. You will have to make several trips to your local courthouse, lose time from work, and, after all that, even if you win a judgment, have difficulty collecting. It is up to you to decide whether to sue or chalk up the whole situation to experience.

Despite all of the foregoing, suing can be relatively easy if you sue in Small Claims Court. Small Claims Court allows you to sue for sums up to usually $1,000. Among common kinds of actions instituted in Small Claims Court are claims against:

- Appliance repairmen for shoddy work, or for failure to perform as agreed
- Garage mechanics and home improvement firms where you believe you have been cheated
- Business firms for the return of cash deposits or to recover damages for breach of contract
- Dry cleaning firms and laundries for damage caused by them to your clothing, drapes, etc.

Those are just an example of some of the claims that may be brought to this court. One important fact to bear in mind is that the only relief afforded a plaintiff in Small Claims is the recovery of money. If, for example, someone or some business firm has wrongfully withheld your property, you cannot sue the defendant in Small Claims to recover the property, although you may sue for the value of the property, providing it is valued within the monetary limits the court deals with. Nor can you bring a Small Claims suit to compel someone to do something or to prevent someone from committing some harm to you or your property. The only result that can be achieved in Small Claims is the recovery of money.

You do not need a lawyer to start a small claims action. You can present your case yourself before the court.

You begin your action by paying a filing fee (usually less than $5) to the clerk, plus the cost of sending a summons by certified mail to the defendant. While at the court, when you are starting the action, you will fill out a form on which you include a brief statement of the facts of your claim against the defendant. You will also have to state the amount of money you seek as damages. When you have completed the form, you will be required to sign it and swear to the truth of its contents in the presence of the clerk. The clerk will tell you the day set for your trial.

On the day of the trial, bring all records and documents pertinent to the case. Some parts of the case can be established by your own testimony, other parts by the testimony of witnesses you may bring.

Remain calm during the trial. If you give in to your feelings, it will not help your case. Do your best to be composed and present your case in a calm and businesslike fashion.

If you win your case and the person still refuses to pay, you must arrange for the services of either a sheriff or a marshal. Both the sheriff and the marshal are legally responsible for enforcing court orders. In most areas, the sheriff is a salaried city employee and the marshal is a private businessman who earns his living by charging a fee to the person for whom he collects the judgment.

25

The Financially
Competent Woman

The aim of this book has been to inform you about money matters so that you can be as knowledgeable as most men in this area; to show you how to organize your personal financial life; and to teach you some of those tricks and techniques that men have known for years.

If you have read this book assiduously and practiced its precepts, you should have achieved these goals. As a financially competent woman, you should be able to check off most of the following:

1. You take a yearly inventory of your net worth and adjust assets and liabilities accordingly.
2. You know how to reconcile your checking account and do it monthly. You can find and correct errors easily. You always have a general idea of how much is in the account.
3. You have made up and tested out a budget for your individual needs. You revise the budget periodically to take into account changing needs. You keep within your budget and thus stay out of debt.
4. You borrow only for necessary reasons and

never more than you can foreseeably pay back.

5. You consider your job not simply as a job but as a stepping stone toward a career goal that you have clearly in mind.

6. You know how to put yourself in line for promotions and raises.

7. You know how to obtain credit and to keep a good credit rating. You know what your credit rights are.

8. You invest a portion of your income to keep ahead of inflation.

9. You know how to read a profit-and-loss statement to keep up with your investments and interests. You know how much your money is earning and when to shift it toward more profitable investments if your money is not earning enough.

10. You have provided insurance for your loved ones and to protect your assets, but you are not insurance-poor.

11. You keep close tabs on your tax deductions, and you keep yourself informed about changes in tax law.

12. If you are a career woman who requires child care, you have chosen the very best you can afford because you consider it an investment in your child's future.

13. You practice good health habits because you realize that prevention keeps down health costs. You have major medical or HMO in case of serious health problems.

14. You know that it is never too early to plan financially for a contented retirement.

15. You know how you stand with Social Security

because you periodically check with your local office as to the status of your account.

16. You have a will drawn up and review it yearly because you want your assets to go to people of your own choosing rather than have the state decide for you. You have provided for the needs of minor children.

17. You know your rights as a consumer and are not hesitant about making complaints in a constructive manner to get redress of your grievance.

18. You have a good, solid money-management team behind you, and you do not hesitate to call on them for advice.

Put this book on a shelf with your other reference books. If you have not been able to check off one or more of the above statements, you will want to reread parts of it to fill in your knowledge.

Glossary of
Money Management Terms

This glossary is meant to introduce you to some of the "buzz words" used in financial affairs. However, it is by no means all-inclusive.

A

Adjusted gross income   On your tax return, income from all sources, minus the following if they apply: moving expenses, employee business expenses, payments to an Individual Retirement Account, payments to a Keogh, interest penalty due to early withdrawal of savings, alimony paid.

Alimony   Separate maintenance or periodic payments of a fixed amount for an indefinite period or payments of an indefinite amount for either a fixed or indefinite period. Does not include child support.

Audit   A systematic investigation of procedures and records to determine conformity with prescribed regulations.

Annual Percentage Rate   The cost of a loan over a full year expressed as a percentage.

Appraisal Fee   The charge for estimating the value of property offered as security.

Asset Property that can be used to repay debt, such as stocks and bonds or a car.

Annuity A sum of money paid annually for life, in return for investment of a specific sum.

B

Balloon Payment A large extra payment that may be charged at the end of a loan or lease.

Basic Educational Opportunity Grant Program (BEOG) Federal government grant that makes funds available to eligible students attending approved colleges or vocational schools.

Balance Sheet A statement showing, in the form of a list, the value of a company's assets and liabilities at a particular date.

Bond A document that binds a person or company or the government to pay a sum of money plus interest at a specific time, in exchange for a certain sum paid by another person, company or government.

Bonus An extra payment in addition to what is expected to be paid.

C

Child Care Credit Twenty percent of expenses that you paid for the care of a child or care of a dependent so that you could be employed. Amount deducted on tax return is limited to $400 for one child; $800 for more than one.

CPA Certified Public Accountant. An accountant who has passed the CPA boards of his state and is qualified to practice in that state preparing financial statements and records.

College Work-Study Program (CWS) Provides jobs for students who have great financial need and must earn a part of their educational expenses at postsecondary institutions.

Commodities Market A market where dealings in commodities can be made, both at national and international levels. Commodities usually are such items as wheat, cotton, sugar, coffee.

Community Property State State in which property is considered owned equally by husband and wife. Community property states are: Arizona, California, Idaho, Louisiana, Nevada, New Mexico, Texas, and Washington.

Common Stock Ordinary stock or shares in a company that does not confer any specific rights or obligations on those who own them.

Convertible Bonds Bonds that may be converted to common stock of the same corporation under certain specified conditions.

Cost of Sales Item on a balance sheet that represents the cost of manufacturing the goods.

D

Debit On a bookkeeping statement, that which is owed.

Debt Service Payment of interest on a debt in addition to the proportion of the principal that is due.

Deferred Annuity An annuity that does not get paid out until some stated future time.

Deficit A deficiency, usually the amount by which liabilities exceed assets.

Depreciation The allowance for diminishing worth due to wear and tear and aging process. Methods of depreciation used on tax returns: straight line method, declining balance method, and sum-of-digits-method.

Dependent On a tax return, a person who qualifies you for the $1,000 exemption if the following five tests are met: (1) support test; (2) gross income test; (3) member of household or relationship test; (4) citizenship test; (5) joint return test.

Decreasing term insurance A type of term insurance under which protection gradually decreases over time.

Dictionary of Occupational Titles (the DOT) Department of Labor publication that details analysis of over 20,000 jobs.

Directory of Consumer Protection and Environmental Agencies Publication by Academic Media, Division of D.A.T.A. It has a subject index in the back of the book that will lead you to the Federal agency you want.

Dividend A part of company profits paid to shareholders at regular intervals.

Double-Entry Bookkeeping A system of bookkeeping whereby the debit and credit of each transaction is recorded.

Dow-Jones Average The average price of certain securities, which are published by the *Wall Street Journal*. They are viewed as significant indicators of business trends.

E

Earned Income Credit Credit applied against your federal tax liability if your earned income or adjusted gross income, whichever is larger, is less than $10,000.

Employee compensation (other than wages, salaries,

tips) On federal tax returns includes fees, commissions, bonuses, disability retirement income, payments to insurance companies not included on your W-2, fair market value of meals and living quarters if given by your employer as a matter of your choice and not for his convenience, strike and lock-out benefits paid by a union from union dues.

Estimated tax The total of your expected income tax and self-employment tax for the following calendar year minus your expected withholding.

Equal Pay Act Act that prohibits discrimination in wage on the basis of sex for jobs that require equal skill, effort, responsibility and that are performed under equal working conditions.

Equal Employment Opportunity Commission Enforces Equal Pay Act.

Extension on Tax Return Taxpayer may get an automatic extension of time to file his income tax return by filing an application on Form 4868 by the return due date. The extension application must show the estimated tax due and be accompanied by check for estimated tax owed. Further extensions will only be allowed for six months from return due date and must be because of severe hardship that prevents filing of a return.

F

Finance Charge The total dollar amount paid to get a loan.

Federal Reserve Banks The central banks of the United States. They hold the cash reserves of the member banks, issue money in the form of bank notes, and provide clearing facilities.

Fixed Assets Assets in the form of land, buildings, etc., that are not readily convertible into cash.

FICA Federal Insurance Contributions Act. Also known as Social Security and also as old age benefits. Includes federal disability benefits and widows' and children's benefits as well as retirement benefits.

Form W-2 Wage and tax statement shows total wages and other compensation paid and the income tax and Social Security tax withheld during the calendar year.

Form W-2P Statement showing the amount of pension or annuity paid during the year and tax withheld on payments.

Form W-4 Form provided employer on which worker indicates marital status and number of withholding allowances claimed.

Full-time student A person who is enrolled for the number of hours or courses considered by the educational organization to be full-time attendance. May be taken as a dependent by parent(s) on tax return if full time for five months of the year, regardless of earnings of student.

G

General Ledger A company's account book that contains a summarized version of all financial transactions.

Guaranteed Student Loan Program (GSL) Enables students to borrow directly from lenders in order to financial educational expenses. Loans are federally insured.

Gross Income All income that is taxed. Excluded from this are: certain specified gifts and inheritances, death benefits, interest on state obligations, certain injury and sickness compensation, and Social Security benefits.

H

Head of Household   Taxpayer who is unmarried on the last day of the tax year and either (1) paid more than half the cost of maintaining a home that is the principal residence for the entire year for a dependent parent; or (2) paid more than half the cost of maintaining a home that is the principal residence for entire year for herself and her unmarried child, grandchild, foster child, stepchild, or other dependent relative.

Health Education Assistance Loan (HEAL)   Federally insured loan made to full-time students pursuing a health-related profession.

Health Maintenance Organization (HMO)   Prepaid health plan that provides comprehensive medical care for a fixed monthly fee.

I

Indemnity   In insurance, means the compensation paid for a loss or injury.

Individual Retirement Arrangement (IRA)   Open to employees who are not covered by a qualified retirement plan. Contributions to IRA may be deducted from gross income. You are allowed to contribute each year the smallest of the following: (1) actual amount of contribution to IRA; (2) $1,500 (3) 15% of your compensation.

Insurance Premium   The payment made by the insured person to the insurance company.

Interest   Sum of money paid for the use of borrowed money.

Investment Credit   On federal tax return a credit of 10% of investment in newly acquired machinery or equipment used in your business. Also may apply to the building of certain property.

J

Joint Account   A savings or credit account signed by two or more people so that all can use the account and all assume liability for it.

Joint Return   Return filed by husband and wife together. You may file a joint return even if one of you had no income or deductions. Both are responsible for the validity of the return.

K

Keogh Plan   Pension plan for self-employed individuals. Individual may contribute 15% of net self-employment income of $7,500 per year, whichever is less, and invest in retirement plan known as Keogh account. The amount of contribution is tax deductible and the earnings are not taxed until withdrawn for retirement income or earlier.

L

Late Payment   A payment made later than agreed upon in a credit contract and on which additional interest may be charged.

Lessee   A person who signs a lease to get temporary use of property.

Lessor   A company that provides temporary use of property, usually in return for periodic payment.

Legacy   A gift of personal property by a will. A bequest.

Legatee   Person who is given a legacy.

Life Insurance Policy Loan   Loan for which you borrow against cash value of your life insurance policy.

Long Term Capital Gain On federal tax return, a gain on the sale or exchange of property held for investment and held for more than one year.

Long Term Capital Loss On federal tax return, a loss on the sale or exchange of capital assets or property held for investment and held more than one year.

M

Maxi-Keogh Pension plan that allows 15% of earnings to be set aside each year or up to $7,500 tax free for that year for self-employed.

Mini-Keogh Pension plan allowing tax free 100% of earnings or $750, whichever is less, for self-employed.

Margin Buying Buying stock on credit through your broker. Broker gives credit and customer makes partial payment for stock. Broker charges interest on costs.

Maximum Tax On federal income tax means the 50% limit on the personal service income of an individual.

Margin Call A call or notice from your broker for money when shares purchased on margin fall below the price that the broker had covered by the client's money.

Minimum Tax An additional tax imposed on taxpayers who have tax preferential items such as accelerated depreciation, stock options, large itemized deductions. This is in addition to regular income tax.

Mutual Funds A medium through which you invest your money in a diversified list of stocks and bonds chosen by professional managers. You buy shares in a mutual fund, which in turn uses your money to buy the securities of other companies.

Money Market A market in which government, corporations, and banks utilize loans for short periods of time.

N

National Direct Student Loans (NDSL) Low-cost federally insured loans for postsecondary institution students.

Net Income Income figure after liabilities have been accounted for.

Net Operating Expense On a corporation balance sheet, it might include selling expenses and general and administrative expenses.

Net Operating Income On a corporation balance sheet, what a corporation has after all operating expenses are deducted from gross profit.

Net Profit Ratio A method of determining the health of a corporation. It is calculated by dividing the net profit by the total income from sales.

Net Worth Total assets minus liabilities.

O

Occupational Outlook Handbook Department of Labor's Bureau of Labor Statistics publication that lists jobs, tells what they are like, what education and training is necessary and what advancement possibilities, earning, and employment outlook is likely to be for those jobs.

Options The right to buy or sell stock within a specified period of time.

Open End Credit A line of credit that may be used over and over again up to a certain borrowing limit. It is also called a charge account or revolving credit.

Open End Lease A lease that may involve a balloon payment based on the value of the property when it is returned.

Overdraft Checking Bank where you have your checking account gives you a line of credit based on your income and net worth against which you may write checks for more money than you have in your account.

Over the Counter When stocks are sold through special dealers rather than through one of the regional or New York or American stock exchanges. The shares are traded between brokerage firms.

P

Passbook Loan Loan for which your savings account passbook is collateral.

Preferred Stocks A stock that is subordinate to the debt a company owes but which has a claim, ahead of the company's common stock, upon the payment of dividends or the assets of the company in the event the company is liquidated.

Profit and Loss Statement Statement that contains an account of profits (or earnings) and loss (the amount by which cost of goods or services relates to the earnings of an organization) for a fixed period of time.

Pyramiding In real estate profits made on one purchase that is made by financing is applied (after current debts are paid) to the purchase of the next acquisition.

R

Reconciliation of Checkbook Process of determining if your bank statement figure and your check book balance figure are identical as of a certain date.

S

Security Interest   The creditor's right to take property or a portion of property offered as security.

Security   Property pledged to the creditor in case of a default on a loan.

Self-employment Tax   Tax on self-employment income. The rate is 8.1% for Old Age and Survivors Benefits and hospitalization. This tax is in addition to regular income tax on self-employment income.

Service Charge   A part of some finance charges, such as the fee for starting an overdraft checking account.

Selling Short   Selling securities on the stock market that you do not have at the time of the sale but must purchase later with the hope that they will be at a lower price than at which one sold short.

Short-Term Capital Gain   A gain on the value or exchange of property held for investment for one year or less.

Short-Term Capital Loss   A loss on the sale or exchange of property or capital assets held for investment and held one year or less.

T

Testator; Testatrix   The person who makes a will is called the testator if a man, and a testatrix if a woman.

Term Insurance   Insurance that covers you for a certain stated period of time.

Tax Credit   An amount used as payment of tax owed.

Tax-Exempt Income   Income that does not have to be included on tax return: Social Security benefits, welfare benefits, life insurance proceeds, armed forces family allotments, nontaxable pensions, nontaxable interest.

Total Support   On federal tax return, to determine

whether you have contributed more than half to the support of a dependent you must first total all support furnished by him, you, and others. Total support encompasses: (1) fair rental value of lodging furnished dependent; (2) all items of expenses paid for the dependent, such as clothing and medical care; (3) a proportionate share of expenses that cannot be attributed directly to the dependent, such as food for the household.

Trust   An agreement whereby the person who established the trust gives property to a trustee to invest and manage for the advantage of the beneficiary.

W

Whole Life Insurance   Unlike term that has a limit on length of coverage it is for your whole life. You may borrow against cash value of the insurance.

Z

Zero Bracket Amount   The amount of deduction built into the tax tables. Itemized deductions are in excess of the zero amount.

Appendix

We came across the following study, *Working Women Speak: Education, Training and Counseling*, in our research for this book and found it too revealing to leave out.

We reproduce here parts of the report on six regional dialogues sponsored by the National Commission on Working Women. The report was prepared for the National Advisory Council on Women's Educational Programs by Cynthia Harrison.

We found the recommendations of the council to the President and Congress are hoped-for goals of many women. Don't forget to read the demurrals, too. They have a great deal of validity.

Characteristics of Dialogue Participants

Total number of participants: 730

AGE	NUMBER	PERCENT
under 25	109	14.9%
26 to 40	362	49.6%

AGE	NUMBER	PERCENT
41 to 55	194	26.6%
56 and over	49	6.7%
unknown	16	2.2%

RACE

	NUMBER	PERCENT
Asian	9	1.2%
Black	163	22.3%
Caucasian	439	60.1%
Hispanic	47	6.4%
Native American	49	6.7%
unknown	23	3.2%

UNION MEMBERSHIP

	NUMBER	PERCENT
yes	312	42.8%
no	376	51.5%
unknown	42	5.8%

OCCUPATION

	NUMBER	PERCENT
clerical	414	56.7%
service	155	21.2%
sales	31	4.2%
operatives	95	13.0%
craft	29	4.0%
unknown	6	0.8%

COMMUNITY

	NUMBER	PERCENT
rural	130	17.8%
urban	382	52.3%
suburban	190	26.0%
unknown	28	3.8%

Recommendations of the Council

I. The Council recommends to the President and the Congress that:

1. Federal anti-discrimination laws (including age discrimination laws) and regulations be enforced more thoroughly by all appropriate agencies to assure that women and girls are afforded educational as well as job equity. Such enforcement should cover career counseling, curriculum selection, classroom training, and postsecondary preparation so that in the future women can be better equipped to avoid the problems of today's working women.

2. effective programs of public information concerning citizens' rights and responsibilities under anti-discrimination laws be undertaken.

3. the Departments of Labor and Health, Education, and Welfare undertake a demonstration program to establish the costs and benefits of stimulating, by tax and other incentives, employer subsidies for employees' education and training. Such a program should cover both job-related and other education, should be designed to facilitate usage by lower level workers, and should analyze the results in terms of productivity and upward mobility.

4. the Departments of Labor and Health, Education, and Welfare undertake a joint effort to provide funds and technical assistance, under existing legislation, to augment local

counseling services for women, within both educational and community settings. Such programs must offer information and assistance concerning the job market, nontraditional occupations, education and training opportunities, financial aid possibilities, childcare and other supportive resources, and individual goal-setting and career planning. They should seek out both employed women and homemakers needing their services.

5. the Federal government support with funds, tax incentives and consultation the establishment of locally-controlled child care centers for all children, including night and summer services.

6. the Federal government extend and publicize its programs for flexible working hours and part-time employment, which would permit women to train for new fields of work.

7. the Federal government establish a policy of hiring para-professionals whenever appropriate.

8. the Department of Labor encourage all employers to formulate and distribute career path manuals for all employees.

II. The Council recommends to the Secretary of Health, Education and Welfare that:

1. legislative definitions be sought which would make less-than-half-time students eligible for Federal student assistance programs.

2. state education agencies and institutions be encouraged to publicize the possibilities for adult students to receive academic credit for lifelong learning experiences, including

academic credit based on demonstrated abilities acquired at work.

3. educational institutions be encouraged to make it possible for all degrees to be earned in classes with flexible hours such as evenings and weekends.

4. funds be provided under discretionary programs to support additional efforts, such as the NCWW Regional Dialogues, intended to foster self-confidence and networking and career-planning skills among working women.

III. Finally, because the needs and problems disclosed by this limited number of working women present major implications for society, the Council urges that the Departments of Health, Education, and Welfare and Labor allocate funds for more comprehensive research on the "80 per cent."

Demurral

Several women at the various Dialogues took exception to the idea that further education represents a fruitful course for working women. "Before additional educational programs, I, personally, and maybe others, need more money," said one delegate.

Dr. Annette Flowers of Towson State University in Maryland said that education and training are often used as a byway: women get more education than they need.

Helen Remmick of the University of Washington pointed out that women with bachelor's degrees earn less than men with eighth grade educations. Women are more likely than men to have high school diplomas, as likely to have A.A. degrees and almost at a par for bachelor's and master's degrees. However, women's educational attainment tends not to translate into job status and pay as men's does.

On-the-job training, a characteristic of higher-paid men's employment, is rarer in women's jobs; women tend to pay to train themselves. But Remmick believes that women's best chances for financial reward lay in getting on-the-job training.

A single mother in Madison echoed her position: "I don't view education (read schooling) as the problem or the solution. Most women who work have learned more than enough on the job to warrant promotions and pay raises without more schooling. Making them go back to school first only provides the employer with yet another method of not dealing with his women employees. After women have started rising in their work setting, then I think talk about further education is applicable."

A woman who had been involved in a WIN program criticized it for initially implying that all women need to get off welfare is training. But, she added, "the program has grown up—employment is where it's at."

Many of the women at the Dialogues expressed a fair level of skepticism about the commitment of the federal, state and local governments to providing equal opportunities: "Thomases promises," said one woman.

A Seattle woman declared with some emotion: "We have seen, in the past few years, a downturn in legislation, in court decisions and in every kind of action on some of the gains made by the struggles of the women's movement from the early 1970's." Pregnancy, seniority, minority and basic human rights are being given short shrift, she said. This Dialogue, she added, will lead to yet another report "that will have all of the relevant information, have all of the sad plight." But the "people in Washington . . . (will) pat us on our heads and say, 'you've really got a long ways to go, baby, but pull yourself up by your socks and keep going.' I think it's a sham!"

Future action will tell if she is right.

THE BEST BUSINESS GUIDES AVAILABLE TODAY FROM PLAYBOY PAPERBACKS

____16784	THE APRIL GAME Diogenes	$2.50
____16721	CHANGE YOUR JOB, CHANGE YOUR LIFE	$1.95
	Arbie M. Dale, Ph.D.	
____16775	THE COMPLETE LIST OF IRS TAX DEDUCTIONS	$2.50
	Rosalie & Howard Minkow	
____16737	CONFESSIONS OF A WALL STREET INSIDER C.C. Hazard	$1.95
____16452	THE FUNNY MONEY GAME Andrew Tobias	$1.95
____16488	GUIDEPOSTS FOR EFFECTIVE SALESMANSHIP	$1.95
	Robert R. Blake & Jane S. Mouton	
____16617	HOW TO BE A SUCCESSFUL EXECUTIVE J. Paul Getty	$2.25
____16613	HOW TO BE RICH J. Paul Getty	$2.25
____16614	HOW TO MAKE MEETINGS WORK	$2.50
	Michael Doyle & David Straus	
____16615	HOW TO SELL YOUR HOUSE FOR MORE THAN	
	IT'S WORTH Jerry Pennington & Fred G. Schultz	$1.95
____16806	THE LANDAU STRATEGY Suzanne Landau & Geoffrey Bailey	$2.50
____16697	LIVING RICH Martin & Diane Ackerman	$2.50
____16616	MASTERY OF MANAGEMENT Auren Uris	$2.25
____16460	MONEY, EGO, POWER Martin & Diane Ackerman	$1.95
____16797	100 SUREFIRE BUSINESSES YOU CAN START	
	WITH LITTLE OR NO INVESTMENT Jeffrey Feinman	$2.50
____16643	PLAYBOY'S INVESTMENT GUIDE Michael Laurence	$2.50
____16645	THE VERY, VERY RICH AND HOW THEY GOT THAT WAY	$2.50
	Max Gunther	
____16465	YOU CAN STILL MAKE IT IN THE STOCK MARKET	$1.95
	Nicholas Darvas	

SELF-HELP BOOKS FROM PLAYBOY PAPERBACKS